5/6/05

Becky,
I bought this
book when I was in
Berkeley last year.
I was looking + reading
some of it tonight +
I thought you might
enjoy it too.
Thanks for your
constant friendship
and for making my
presence at my
grandson's birth
possible.
Love,
Linda

FRIENDSHIP
A PIECE OF FOREVER

FRIENDSHIP

A PIECE OF FOREVER

SELECTED PROSE AND POETRY

Edited by

MARY ANNE HUDDLESTON, I.H.M.

THE PILGRIM PRESS
CLEVELAND, OHIO

The Pilgrim Press, Cleveland, Ohio 44115
© 1999 by Mary Anne Huddleston

Printed in the United States of America on acid-free paper

04   03   02   01   00   99   5   4   3   2   1

Library of Congress Cataloging-in-Publication Data

Friendship : a piece of forever : selected prose and poetry / edited by Mary
    Anne Huddleston.
        p.   cm.
      ISBN 0-8298-1349-7 (alk. paper)
      1. Friendship Literary collections.   I. Huddleston, Mary Anne.
    PN6071.F7F75   1999
    808.8'0353—dc21   99-28649
                                                                  CIP

To
the friends
who,
    like fine liqueurs,
        set my spirit tingling.

open your heart:
i'll give you a treasure
of tiniest world
a piece of forever . . .

—e. e. cummings

CONTENTS

PART THREE: IMPRESSIONS

PREFACE

We do not know why one heart greets another
As though an alchemy had made them one.
In understanding bright as it is sudden,
It has been dusk and then there is the Sun.

—Helen Welsheimer, "Heart to Heart"

❧

LATENT IN THESE LYRIC VERSES are the quintessential elements of friendship, the first two lines stressing as they do how inexplicable this relationship is. And it is inexplicable because, although we may experience the exultant joy of friendship, we cannot comprehend the why and the how of it. Yet the longing to penetrate its mystery goes on and on.

When bookshelves the world over are weighted with poetry and prose on this subject, why another friendship anthology? My principal answers are two: first, as one of the noblest of human relationships, if not the noblest, friendship can alleviate the pernicious and pervasive loneliness of our day. This being true, a fresh approach to friendship, which this book aims to be, would seem appropriate. The second reason for this book is that testimonials to the riches of friendship likewise attest to its reality. Perhaps, then, this anthology will help to reclaim the reality of friendship for those postmodernists who doubt its existence. Such is the *raison d'être* for *Friendship—a Piece of Forever.*

What is the notion of friendship that undergirds the choices for this book? Notions of friendship abound. The one presented here is my own, the culmination of years of labor to put friendship into words. In a sense, it is a futile effort, for friendship defies articulation. Still, if we are to talk about it, it is a necessary effort. As I have come to know it,

friendship
is
the unself-seeking, reciprocal love
evoked in two persons
by their inexplicable attraction to each other,
and
manifested in

> trust,
>
> reverence,
>
> candor,
>
> freedom,
>
> forbearance,
>
> intimacy,
>
> and
>
> delight in each other's presence.

This formulation reflects the complexity of friendship and also its sun and shadow sides. Because it is not the conventional notion of friendship, it calls for some commentary.

That friendship is unself-seeking love occasions little controversy. Neither does the idea of reciprocal love, though traditionally the term "mutual" has been used. "Reciprocal," however, seems a better choice, for no relationship is really fifty-fifty (and no two persons are really equals). Some may complain that "service" belongs in any definition of friendship, but this omission is not an oversight. Rather, it is a recognition that love, of which friendship is a form, implies or includes service, for love instinctively ministers to the needs of others. Moreover, in some situations, such as imprisonment, illness, and geographical separation, friends are simply not able to serve one another. Yet who would say that friendship is not possible in these circumstances?

With respect to the manifestations of friendship, the first five elements are generally accepted, although some readers may prefer different words—for example, tolerance for forbearance, honesty for candor, and so forth. The elements that are questionable to some are the last two, namely, intimacy and delight in each other's presence.

Intimacy is problematic for some, because they wrongly identify it as genital only. Although genital intimacy, when moral, is admissible in friendship, the intimacy proper to friends is much broader. It means the level of rapport that allows one to confide one's convictions, desires, feelings, fantasies, failures, successes, etc.—the deep-down thoughts and experiences that usually resist revelation. It is this latter intimacy that is germane to friendship.

Integral to friendship as intimacy is, it is not what distinguishes friendship from universal or neighbor love *(agápe)*. The distinguishing element is delight in each other's presence, and experience bears this out: the cantankerous or boring neighbor, whom we are making every effort to love, never evokes in us the delight that even a brief meeting with a friend occasions.

Besides distinguishing friendship from universal love, it is this delight that inspires novelists, dramatists, and poets to creative heights. It might have been one such experience that moved Katherine Phillips to write:

> Friendship is abstract of love's noble flame.
>> 'Tis love refined and purged of all its dross,
> 'Tis next to angel's love, if not the same . . .

While some might appreciate the poet's lyricism, they likewise might contend that emphasis on delight in friendship is a denial of its shadow side. Certainly friendship is not unadulterated bliss, but, even if its joy is intermittent, it is real, and it is unparalleled in human experience. In fact, Pierre Teilhard de Chardin asserted that friendship was part of what enabled him to endure the torment of suppression that he suffered for a number of years.

Thus far, this preface has been an attempt to articulate the notion of friendship underlying the preparation of this anthology. It is now time to give some explanation for the choice and arrangement of the selections in the book. The choices were made irrespective of a given author's or poet's gender, race, nationality, religion, or professional or social status. Many of the selections reflect Christian tenets, but this is by happenstance, not by design. All selections appear here as found in print in book, journal, or original manuscript;

no substantive corrections have been made, though some minor changes in punctuation have been made for the sake of clarity and consistency. Nor has there been an attempt to edit for sexist language, for in my judgment, to alter texts is to distort the historical record and likewise to violate authentic scholarship. Some selections are long, some short. Completeness of thought rather than length has been the criterion for their inclusion.

To avoid subjecting the reader to reruns, effort has been made to select most entries from the twentieth century. Similarly, there has been effort to achieve a balance in feminine and masculine authorship.

In a review of the selections, a pattern seemed to emerge. Accordingly, the book has three sections: Part One, Perspectives—philosophizing about friendship; Part Two, Realities—actual recorded experiences of friendship; and Part Three, Impressions—brief keynotes on friendship by seven notable men and women.

It is my fond hope that the selections will lend themselves to savoring rather than dissection, and that, in turn, savoring will yield fresh insight into and renewed desire for this cherished relationship (the "elixir of life"). Then, too, the savoring should better dispose readers for friendship, both continuing and new.

Preparation of this manuscript has been, for me, akin to a long retreat during which I have experienced humble and deepening gratitude for the friendships granted me. I find myself repeating, almost like a mantra, the words of Jesus, son of Sirach (Sirach 6:14–16):

A faithful friend is a sturdy shelter:
      he that has found one has found
           a treasure.
There is nothing so precious
      as a faithful friend; . . .
A faithful friend is an elixir of
      life.

May we, readers and editor alike, *be* and *be blessed with* faithful friends.

ACKNOWLEDGMENTS

THERE IS A TRUISM found in many acknowledgments and, of necessity, repeated here, namely, "It is impossible to thank by name all who have helped to bring about the publication of this book." Nevertheless, to some persons, my indebtedness is so great that I must try to cite them, even at the risk of offending others by omission.

For all sorts of reasons, I am deeply indebted to the leadership of my religious congregation, Sisters, Servants of the Immaculate Heart of Mary of Monroe, Michigan, and to the following individuals: Sisters Hilda Bonham, Marie Gerald Murphy, Claudia Carlen, Christa De Primo, and Jane Mary Howard; the Rev. Msgr. H. Gil Weil, the Reverends Stephen Rooney, Ronald Chocol, Howard Gray, S.I., and Michael Proterra, S.J.; and Carol Richards Sharpe and Robert S. Huddleston, the latter being the mainstay of the actual preparation of this manuscript.

Not every author has had my good fortune of the combined expertise and consideration of the editorial staff of Pilgrim Press: Timothy Staveteig, editor; Marjorie Pon, associate publisher; and Kelley Baker, editorial assistant. Kelly, incidentally, has gone far beyond the call of duty in her efforts to help. Likewise, the assistance of reference librarians, especially Carl Katafiasz of the Ellis Branch of the Monroe County Library and Mary Nash of Reinert Alumni Memorial Library of Creighton University, Omaha, Nebraska, has been invaluable.

In fine, it is with a very grateful heart that I acknowledge all the pertinent contributions of named and unnamed acquaintances, relatives, and friends.

PART ONE

PERSPECTIVES

❧

Let's start by talking about friendship—the warmth, intimacy, affection, joy, obligations, need, jealousy, sorrow, sharing, loving, and why we need and want this central experience of our lives affirmed and articulated.

—Susan Koppelman, *Women's Friendships*

Love and Friendship
Emily Brontë

Love is like the wild rose-briar,
Friendship is like the holly-tree—
The holly is dark when the rose-briar blooms
But which will bloom most constantly?

The wild rose-briar is sweet in spring,
Its summer blossoms scent the air;
Yet wait till winter comes again
And who will call the wild-briar fair?

Then scorn the silly rose-wreath now
And deck thee with the holly's sheen,
That when December blights thy brow
He still may leave thy garland green.

❧

The Power of Love
Robert O. Johann, S.J.

MUCH HAS BEEN WRITTEN about love. But most of the writing, as Père Teilhard de Chardin has remarked, concerns "only the sentimental face of love, the joy and miseries it causes us." Relatively little has been set down about love as a way of life. And the power of love, which is the power of Being itself, has been all but passed over.

Some inkling of love's power can be had by each of us if we but recall those rare and privileged moments when, with sudden splendor, the brightness of love burst into our lives.

There we were, wrapped up with ourselves and lost in a seemingly indifferent world. We had allowed ourselves to become harassed by care and anxiety, absorbed with our immediate preoccupations, oppressed by the bleak business of coping with every day. Then suddenly the veil lifted. Through a chance encounter, an unexpected kindness, the sheer radiance of a loving glance, all the more precious because unhoped for and unmerited, Being beckoned to us. However momentarily, we caught a glimpse of the world beyond care. We came alive. Possibilities for existing in ways we had forgotten, in ways that made our past routines appear a barren desert—possibilities that summoned forth a creativity we did not know we had, that infinitely enriched our present by holding up to us a future without bounds—newly quickened our minds and hearts. Even a moment in love's presence awakened us to life and we knew the truth in Wilhelmsen's beautiful phrase: "What being-*loved* makes being do is precisely *be.*"

Of course, the moment was quickly gone; the humdrum resumed its sway. But we make an abiding mistake if we assume that, because the exaltation did not last—indeed, in a world frayed by time, could not last—we did not really see anything, that it was all illusion. Love's moment, even if only remembered, has a message for us. It speaks to us about ourselves and discloses within us a capacity and power that, but for love's revelation, we might never have come to know.

The reason why an encounter with love moves us so deeply is that, no matter how humble and fleeting the gesture that embodies it, it dramatically recalls to us our own vocation as persons. For the person is not a mere element caught up in nature's restless process. His role and significance cannot be measured simply in terms of specific endowments and needs or the relative place he occupies in some larger scheme. In the person, the transcendent power and creative freedom of God Himself are unleashed in their own right. To be a person is to share in Being itself and in Being's creative concern for all that is. It is to have and exercise Being's power to cherish something for its own sake, regardless of return. The person who lives as a person is the one in whom that pure devotion-to-being which *is* Being has gained untrammeled sway and shines forth in every deed. He is the one who has learned that to be is to love, to spend oneself for others that they may more truly be, and that in the spending one is not impoverished but ever more deeply rooted in that limitless abundance on which one draws.

This is the secret of love's power over us. To be loved is to encounter Being itself, eternity in time, God's face among the faces of men. The loving person translates for our benefit the exuberant life of God in human terms. He gives us a glimpse of that boundless benevolence that has sustained us from the beginning, despite our heedlessness, and that seeks this very moment to erupt in our lives and organize them anew in its own image. In the one who loves us, we hear God's voice in the realm of everyday, are newly reminded of His abiding call that defines our existence as persons and with exquisite patience awaits our free response. The only thing is not to let it go unanswered.

For the vision, I have suggested, is brief. The gracious presence is abruptly withdrawn, soon consumed by death or distance, swept away by the rush of events. What was disclosed is once more concealed. Being itself, having relied on this encounter to solicit our love, quickly recedes behind the manifold determinations of everyday. And then it is only too easy to think we saw nothing at all.

The power of love, therefore, although it is the power of Being itself, is not overpowering. It intermittently stirs us, rouses us, awakens us—but it respects our freedom. Blessed is the man who recognizes it when it visits him and lets it transform his life. For only he can know what it means *to be*. 🌿

Friendship
L. Vander Kerken

AUTHENTIC FRIENDSHIP of a high order calls for an uncommon endowment in mind and in heart, a rich endowment but one which may make a man vulnerable, too; it culminates in a free openness and liberality of the person's whole being. Such a friendship is made possible by what one might call a feeling for friendship. For there is a feeling for friendship as there is a feeling for art, for poetry, for organization, and so on. This feeling is a special power of empathy for all that concerns the object of the feeling; it is also a special power of discernment permitting one to distinguish, even in the most obscure borderline cases, what is authentic from what is not. It is an insight into the nature of things, a realization of their extraordinary value, and an ability to express oneself graciously and spontaneously in words and actions. Above all, having a feeling for something implies that one likes, finds pleasure in, exercising this feeling for its own sake. Thus there are people who have a feeling for friendship, "who love to love." Others lack this feeling, as they may lack a feeling for music, for nature, and even for truth. Or at least such a feeling remains rudimentary. Such a lack consists simply in "not seeing"; it is like the absence of a sense, but it is not recognized as an absence, for the awareness of the absence would presuppose the presence of the feeling.

The feeling for friendship shows a strong analogy with the feeling for happiness; to a great extent, the two coincide. The feeling for happiness also is a special aptitude for being happy, the capacity for finding the source of happiness everywhere, even in the minutest events of life; especially the disposition for putting happiness above all else. Strange as it may sound, that feeling, too, is lacking in many people. They have a feeling for fun, for pleasure, for the satisfaction found in wealth and power, but they have no real capacity for simply feeling happy on account of their happiness itself.

The connection between friendship and happiness consists in the fact that "being happy" means essentially, "being happy with." Happiness as a merely individual possession will soon fade for want of the "reflection" whereby the person sees his happiness reflected in the happiness of another person. But this reflection is not mere *knowledge*. It is a *bringing about* of the mutual happiness by mutual communication. Especially in the sphere of happiness a man really possesses only what he gives to others. This is true in all the forms of personal love, but in friendship most particularly.

But friendship is not exempt from the relative character of everything human. However undivided, sincere and faithful it may be, it is bound to discover in itself a certain inability to give itself to the limit. Thus in friendship, too, there revives—more intensely in proportion as the friendship is deeper—the fundamental loneliness of man as man. Yet in this existential loneliness, the awareness of the bond of friendship is both strong and strengthening, and undoubtedly the common reflection of the mutual solitude itself lightens the burden of this solitude, although it would be an illusion to expect that it might ever completely free man of his loneliness. The reason for this is that man's deepest loneliness derives from the transcendence of his nature. This nature is ultimately a "loneliness for God." That is why it also has a positive meaning. As "loneliness for" it turns into an *expecting* and an *abiding,* a hopeful looking for something great that is to come. This positive aspect of loneliness too is shared in love and friendship, it can be held in common because it is something positive. Expecting becomes expecting together. In this expecting together human love and friendship fulfill their ultimate potentiality.

In the light of this perspective the event which seems to break up the friendship, the death of one of the friends, becomes as it were a consecration of this friendship. One of them at least has now overcome loneliness, even though this may make the loneliness of the surviving friend more oppressive. Yet over this loneliness is diffused a gentle light, emanating from a deeper knowledge that for one of them the great communion has begun. He has led the way. And he remains invisibly present to his friend, he awaits him, knowing that before long both of them will be joined in a friendship which is forever. ❧

A Thing beyond Compare
Charles Davis

THERE ARE FEW MORE REVEALING SIGNS of the failure of Christians than the corruption of the word "charity." It originally expressed the heart of the Christian message, but it has become so degraded in meaning as to be unusable except in a carefully prepared context. It should evoke the generous and personal love of God for men, the joyful response on man's part, and the loving personal relations that knit all men together in Christ. Instead, what are its associations? A cold, impersonal almsgiving, a material giving used to excuse a refusal of the person as a person, a pretended higher love of those who, humanly speaking, are cheerfully loathed. Uncharitableness chiefly means gossip; to be an object of charity is to be in a sorry state. Such is the semantic history of Christian love.

The Christian ideal is difficult, and failure not surprising. But I think a particular cause of the distressing deviation underlying the destruction of the word "charity" is the neglect of the human basis of Christian love. Christian love strengthens and transforms human love; it does not replace it. The human analogue of charity is friendship. Only from the experience and appreciation of friendship as a human value can we understand and rise to Christian love.

In the sapiential books of the Old Testament we have an inspired record of the practical human wisdom of the ancient East. The Book of Ecclesiasticus has noted the worth of genuine friendship: "True friendship, sure protection and rare treasure found; true friendship, a thing beyond compare, its tried loyalty outweighing gold and silver; true friendship, elixir of life, and of life eternal!" (6:14–16). Friendship we all prize. And, unfortunately, we all, too, have to lament its rarity.

Poets and psychologists, novelists and philosophers, are needed to set forth the meaning of friendship. May a brief remark not seem jejune! Through mutual communication and exchange, friends form themselves into a single, lovingly conscious subject for human living. What they communicate is principally what they are, not what they know. They disclose themselves to each other. They do this less by discourse, more by familiar dealings with each other. And each learns to know himself through reflection in the response of the other. Such communication both demands and leads to a mutual sharing and giving in the activities and responsibilities of life and in the possessions and fruits it brings.

Such coming together of two or more persons is prevented by selfishness or greed, by fear, by the inadequacy that seeks security in submission or domination. Positively, it springs from the same openness by which man goes beyond himself to accept God or is at least on the road to finding Him.

Christ came to offer man friendship with the Father through friendship with Himself: "The Father himself is your friend, since you have become my friends" (John 16:27). He accepted the requirement of self-disclosure: "I do not speak of you any more as my servants; a servant is one who does not understand what his master is about, whereas I have made known to you all that my Father has told me; and so I have called you my friends" (15:15). He wanted all His disciples to be united together in such friendship: "This is my commandment, that you should love one another, as I have loved you" (15:12).

But is not a universal friendship a contradiction? In a sense, yes. The limitations of our human condition mean that we cannot achieve actual friendship except with a few. We cannot escape, as men, differences of knowledge and temperament, of background and interest, of age and experience; we cannot even meet more than a few people sufficiently often for friendship to be possible. Again, the mutual relation of friendship is feasible only if the other person is able and willing to take up our offer.

But particular friendships, far from being inimical to charity, are the soil in which it grows. We must learn to love some people fully as friends, if our profession of love for all men is not to be a meaningless abstraction. Charity in fact means that we regard all men as potential friends. In other words, we so honor them as persons and will their good that we show that we would gladly accept them as friends had we the ability, time and opportunity to overcome the obstacles. But to do this we must know what achieved friendship means by experiencing it. Charity cannot purify and extend, deepen and give fresh motives to human love, where human love is stunted and repressed. The fear of even open and healthy particular friendships in religious life is more likely to produce people incapable of loving anyone than saints loving everyone. Would we rebuke Jesus for his special affection for John?

What is Christian rests upon the human. To attempt to by-pass the human in the name of a higher spirituality is to prevent the Christian enhancement from emerging into reality. The history of the word "charity" might have been different had Christians been more human. ❧

A Note on Friendship
Caryll Houselander

I AM UP NOW, and the pneumonia is cleared up, but I admit I have never in my life felt more like something well chewed that the cat has brought in. But it's nice to be able to stay alone in my warm room and write: my work is behindhand and in chaos, so I hope for comparative solitude to get on with it. Unfortunately, however, people are now pestering to come and see me again, and some of them have. When they do come they all declare I look the picture of health, and obviously do not believe that I have had pneumonia at all! . . .

A very interesting and unusually nice Mohammedan, who has become very interested in Catholicism through reading *Guilt*, called on Saturday. He wanted a full and exhaustive exposition of the doctrine of the Blessed Trinity from me—a thing I find taxes every ounce of mental concentration at the best of times. I wished Frank or Maisie had been there. Anyhow, I was able to persuade him to read *Theology and Sanity*.

I am terribly glad that you are feeling more at peace and have found happiness in your two new friendships. But I feel that one tiny word of advice is needed. I am convinced that they both are as good and beautiful in character as you think, and from S.'s letter, enclosed, as well as from what you tell me, she is very wise too. But the warning is this: do not ask from any human being that which God only can give. I grant you that God gives Himself *through* human beings and unites Himself through human relationships, provided the people involved realize their human relationships as a mutual giving and receiving of Christ-life and the Holy Spirit, and do nothing to frustrate this. But God does not give Himself wholly through any *one* friend, lover, husband, or what not: I mean rather that although every real friendship is a mutual Christ-giving, no one friend can give God to you so perfectly as completely to satisfy and fill your need for His love.

Human elements enter into *every* human relationship, and disturb the serenity of them all sometimes. You see, we all tend to ask from the other human being things that God alone can give and we can only attain by a mutual and conscious turning to God together, and accepting from God together whatever suffering is the condition of love—and of course suffering in *some* measure is the condition of all love and every love. Take, for example, security, in the sense of being certain that nothing will ever come between oneself and the friend—that they will never be taken away. Well, one *knows* that to try and think so is sheer escapism; you, my dear, know it all too well. Every happy husband and wife *must* be secretly haunted, especially as they grow older, by the knowledge that one or the other will die first and the other will be left alone. No matter how many friends or children they have, no one will ever be able to fill the place in their soul of the one who has gone. . . .

God's love for those we love is infinitely greater than our own, and it is as well to remember it, and to remember it especially when He allows things to happen which threaten both their happiness or safety, and ours.

And it is also the ultimate reason why, despite the Christ-giving element in our relationships, they can never be perfect here. There must be empty places left in our hearts, because the final happiness of both depends upon God Himself possessing us completely: once that is achieved, heaven can begin for both, and in heaven of course, unlike here, our friendships will take part, not only imperfectly, in God, but perfectly.

That, however, won't happen here; so, while thanking God for the joy and miracle of your new friendships, do not demand perfection of them, and do not be disappointed when trials arise. Actually, but for the failure of other relationships in your life, and for the suffering you have had through them, which by the by you have borne with magnificent fortitude and sweetness, but for those things you would not now be ready, fashioned as it were by the hammer of God, for these friendships. ❦

Can Women and Men Be Friends?
Caroline J. Simon

"MEN AND WOMEN CAN'T BE FRIENDS—because the sex part always gets in the way," says Harry, one of the title characters of the popular film *When Harry Met Sally*. The amount of discussion the film caused shows that its leading question is compelling. Millions of viewers wanted to know, can women and men be friends?

The film's question is raised in the context of the social shifts that have opened new possibilities for serious, but nonromantic, relationships between the sexes. Social barriers between the sexes have crumbled. "Woman's place" is no longer exclusively in the home but in the factory, the lab, the seminar room and the boardroom. In many families the shared task of "parenting" is creating common ground for men and women as it replaces "mothering" as a woman's primary focus.

C. S. Lewis observed in *The Four Loves* that "in most societies at most periods Friendship will be between men and men or between women and women. The sexes will have met one another in Affection and Eros but not in this love. For they will seldom have had with each other the companionship in common activities which is the matrix of Friendship." But in modern America the issue has become moot. Men and women do share in common activities. We are in a position to test Gilbert Meilaender's hunch that "friendship between the sexes may take us not out of ourselves but beyond ourselves and may make us more whole, balanced and sane than we could otherwise be." Perhaps it is time to take seriously such questions as: What is the nature of male-female friendship? Does it differ in significant ways from same-gender friendship? How do male-female friendships differ from romances and marital loves?

The need to explore these questions is urgent; given present realities, many men and women will naturally develop affectionate relationships outside of marriage. These new possibilities for intergender friendship present opportunities; they also present risks. Unless those risks are squarely faced, "the sex part" of the interactions between men and women is likely to cause more pain and muddle than balance or sanity.

Wallace Stegner's novel *Crossing to Safety* makes passing references to this subject. Larry, the narrator, reflects on the friendship between his wife and another woman: . . .

> What I am sure of is that friendship—not love, friendship—is as possible between women as between men, and that in either case it is often stronger for not having to cross sexual picket lines. Sexuality and mistrust often go together, and both are incompatible with *amicitia*.

Larry claims that friendship is just as possible between two women as between two men. However, by implication at least, he seems to claim that between a heterosexual man and a heterosexual woman, friendship is problematic, if not downright impossible. Having to cross sexual picket lines weakens friendship, says Larry, and sexuality and friendship are incompatible. Because few interactions between men and women are completely devoid of potential sexual undertones, the conclusion would seem to be that deep friendships between men and women are precluded. Larry, it seems, agrees with Harry: the sex part always gets in the way.

Friendship and romantic love are distinctive but not incompatible and certainly are found together in some marriages. In such cases sexuality sets no picket line but is, rather, one of the threads that binds the partners together. It can do so, of course, because a good marriage is a place where sexuality and mistrust are not linked. Similarly, sexuality will be incompatible with friendship only to the extent that sexuality is linked with mistrust.

Traditionally, Christianity has projected an ideal of community in which men and women, unless they have some special calling to celibacy, make and unfailingly keep vows of sexual exclusivity. Christians are to say to one other person, "You and I will be stitched together by a thousand threads of feeling and shared experience. Moreover, the thread of full sexual expression will connect me to you and you alone. Other threads of shared experience will connect me to others, but not the sexual one; the threads with which I am connected with others will never be allowed to threaten our connection." A community formed around such commitments would be a safe space for marriage, family and friendship, without segregating the sexes. Men and women could be friends, both inside and outside marriage, without trying to be asexual; friendships between men and women could be healthy and unproblematic without the friends pretending to be genderless. In such a world sexuality would not set up picket lines because sexuality and mistrust would *not* frequently go hand in hand. In such a community sexuality would not be incompatible with *amicitia*.

American society is obviously not such a community. Such a community is an *idea* in the Kantian sense—that is, a pattern that is nowhere perfectly realized, but to which we can and should aspire. To the extent that the church seeks to be the in-breaking of the kingdom of God, it is a pattern for Christian community. The world, in the Pauline sense of that term, will give us precious little help in pursuing this ideal, but it is the ideal toward which Christians should be helping one another strive. It is an ideal against which one aspect of the sacramental nature of marriage vows can be understood. Such vows, if they can be rested upon, create a space in which sexuality and mistrust need not be linked, in which the blessing of safety is spread beyond the circle of the marriage to the broader community.

Apart from such a sacrament, every thread that links men and women beyond their marriages is a potential threat to the marriage. In such a setting Larry and Harry are surely right: men and women will not be able to be close friends. The question "Are we becoming too close?" will haunt them. Such a question really means, Am I likely to sacrifice my marriage and family for this other relationship? In a world where the answer could be yes, intimacy between men and women outside marriage will always be a risk.

The potential problems of intergender friendships should not be minimized, especially in our culture. Ours is about as far as one can get from a society in which breaking vows is unthinkable, so such friendships will always involve risk and, most likely, some degree of mistrust and self-doubt. However, Christians believe that through grace we can strive not to be conformed to this world. Grace gives us the permission, and perhaps in some cases a mandate, to run such risks and to aspire to the "innocent intimacy" of friendship between the sexes.

The word *mandate* here may seem inappropriately strong. However, if one considers the alternatives to creating space for "innocent intimacy" between the sexes, it does not seem outlandish to talk this way. Until fairly recently in the West, and up to the present in many other cultures, the roles of women have been severely restricted by the idea that if men and women who are not married to one another are thrown into situations of social contact, illicit sexual relations are the predictable outcome. Modern Western culture has not produced counterevidence to that view; rather, for the most part, it has chosen to wink at, smirk at or endorse illicit sexuality. This provides evidence that an agenda for women that is both Christian and feminist may be possible only if innocent intimacy is possible. The "picket fences" of sexual mistrust and self-doubt interfere not only with friendship, but also with collegiality and mentorship between men and women in professional settings.

Simone Weil's definition of friendship in *Waiting for God* is especially apt for characterizing what intergender friendships committed to innocent intimacy would be like. Weil believes that the natural consequence of desiring a relationship with another is a desire to control. She contrasts such natural situations with those made possible by grace, and claims that "friendship is a miracle by which a person consents to view from a certain distance, and without coming any nearer, the very being who is as necessary to him as food. It requires the strength of soul that Eve did not have; and yet she had no need of the fruit. If she had been hungry at the moment when she looked at the fruit, and if in spite of that she had remained looking at it indefinitely without taking one step toward it, she would have performed a miracle analogous to that of perfect friendship."

Even if the desire to "take over" or "be taken over by" those whom we care deeply about is not an inviolable psychological law, it is a familiar and widespread human tendency, perhaps especially (given cultural forces) in male-female relationships. "Standing at a distance" from our friends, those whose fortunes we identify with ours, may not literally be a miracle, but anyone who has lived for any length of time will know that it can be a very difficult feat. It is the distance at which one stands that marks the difference between friendship, romantic love and marital love.

Robert Solomon claims that love is a dialectic between an ideal of merger or shared identity and one of individuation. This applies to the *we* of marital love and to intergender friendship. Both of these kinds of love involve a tension between union and shared identity, on the one hand, and autonomy and independence on the other. In both of these kinds of love, the tension between these opposing forces must be kept in balance; what distinguishes the nature of a *we* from the nature of friendship is the appropriate placement of the fulcrum that strikes the balance. As romantic love moves toward marital love, the fulcrum that strikes the creative balance within love's dialectic is not at the center, but toward the side of union. In friendship the fulcrum is much farther toward the side of individuation.

In marital love imagination produces insight into a joint destiny; in friendship imagination produces insight into the creative tension that allows the friends to endorse and contribute to one another's destinies (which will include, if they are both married, their respective joint destinies with their spouses), while not allowing any existing sexual undertones to impel them toward union. What makes intergender friendship distinctive is the nature of the balancing, necessitated by social, emotional and biological factors, to keep it from transmuting into romantic or marital love. This balancing generates a tension that can itself be creative.

The risks involved in the tensions within friendship between the sexes can be a spur to prayerful reliance on grace; they may also be a cause for stumbling. It is best to be fully cognizant of potential problems. Such cognizance will lead some to pursue intergender friendship with the appropriate mixture of gratitude and caution; it may lead others to conclude that such friendship is not their "calling."

C. S. Lewis asserts that "the sex part" makes friendship between the sexes naturally gravitate toward romantic love: "When the two people who thus discover that they are on the same secret road are of different sexes, the friendship which arises between them will very easily pass—may pass in the first half-hour—into erotic love. Indeed, unless they are physically repulsive to each other or unless one or both already loves elsewhere, it is almost certain to do so sooner or later." If Lewis is correct here, it would mean that vows of fidelity to another or vows of chastity are not only compatible with friendship between men and women but are a necessary condition for such friendship.

Two sorts of doubts might be raised about Lewis's view. One might question whether all friends feel the pull toward union to the same extent and whether this pull, if it is felt, will be experienced as erotic desire. People's libidos *do* vary, after all, and this seems a separate issue from that of whether the friends "are physically repulsive to each other." Moreover, friends may have reasons other than vows for resisting any pull that they do feel toward union. For example, two friends, though unattached, may see one another's destinies clearly enough to know that any joint destiny they might share is unlikely to enhance each one's personal flourishing. Under such circumstances one might make sure that the balance within the relationship remains tilted toward individuation out of love for one's friend.

Those who suspect that attempting intergender friendship is naïve and reckless will have a different sort of objection to Lewis's claim. Loving elsewhere, and being committed elsewhere by vows of fidelity or chastity, may seem too flimsy a barrier to the pull of our embodied natures toward experiencing strong emotions as erotic and toward their sexual expression in intergender relationships. Remembering Shakespeare's line from *The Tempest,* such an objector might say, "The strongest oaths are straw to the fire in the blood."

There are two other potential problems that should also be noted. The first is nonsexual jealousy, and the second is nonsexual rivalry. Even if a friendship succeeds in sustaining innocent intimacy, it may still cause problems of jealousy for the friends' spouses. Psychological research shows that not all jealousy is sexual. Although men most often worry that their partners may think a potential rival is a superior sexual partner, many women are as worried over their husband's finding another woman easier to talk to or her personality more captivating as they are about sexual rivalry per se. In cases of such nonsexual jealousy, knowing that one's husband is not sexually involved with his friend (and is not going to be) will not be of much comfort.

Finally, even when jealousy is not a problem, attention must be paid to how a friendship affects the dynamics within the marriages, if any, of the friends. Marriages in which there is healthy communication and active affection between the spouses are unlikely to be threatened by a friendship. On the other hand, if there are other stresses on the marriage, or if the reason for pursuing a friendship is some perceived lack within the marriage itself, friendship may exacerbate existing problems.

Friendship should not be allowed to undermine the "presence" of the friends within their marriages. One must guard against infidelity to one's marriage, and not all infidelity is sexual. John C. Haughey is correct in observing in *Should Anyone Say Forever?* that

> being faithful means, for starters, being fully present in the relational situation in which one finds oneself. The faithful person lives facing into a "we are" horizon. . . . Communion is not a state of being that one enters and sleeps in. It is a dynamic of interrelationships that must be constantly nurtured. Fidelity involves being willing to generate the ingenuity needed to nurture the communion that is already present (or hoped for). . . . The faithful person is one who continues to center his or her heart. Faithful persons do not cease to resituate themselves in the communion they are in.

Imagination's insight cannot be indifferent to the flourishing of the *we* of a married friend, for its flourishing is integral to the friend's destiny. An intergender "friendship" that is blind to the good of the friend's *we* is fiction-making's counterfeit for friendship. It amounts to flirtatious ego-gratification or a quasi-affair. Such relationships involve no joyful renunciation, but are dangerous self-deception.

One area in which self-deception may be especially problematic concerns the physical expression of affection. In her book *Celibate Passion,* Janie Gustafson gives a frank treatment of this issue. Deploring the fact that fear of vulnerability tends to make us "rubberize" our existence, she aspires to articulate a way of being psychologically intimate and passionate that can be practiced in various intergender relationships. She broadens the concept of celibacy, applying her concept of celibate passion to intimate connections between people who have actually taken vows of celibacy (unmarried people and rare married couples who have made this decision) and between people who are married, but not to each other.

Celibate passion is Gustafson's recommended alternative to a view of sexuality that she sees as both utilitarian and centered on libido. She characterizes what she takes to be the prevailing attitude: "Everything in our present mentality is geared toward progression toward orgasm. It is both sad and terribly uncreative, I think, that so many of us believe that love must be expressed by the full completion of this succession." If we give up the utilitarian idea that all physical expression is a stage on the way to intercourse, we can, she says, replace strict and rigid restrictions on physical contact in our relationships with "purposeless and leisurely" physical expressions that are meant as intrinsic vehicles of intimacy rather than as foreplay.

She cites, as examples of noncoital intimacy, scenarios from courtly romantic love where partners indulged in "protracted sessions of sex play" while deliberately refraining from intercourse. Although she says she is not suggesting that

23

such behavior would "always be appropriate and moral in a relationship between any man and woman," she also hopes that celibate passion can be "fully sensuous and spontaneously tactile." Rigid standards, then, should be replaced by wise personal judgment:

> I do not think that persons who have realized the celibate part of themselves and who then happen to fall in love with each other, can with full integrity just fall into bed. How far they go in physical expression and what they do together must be a deliberate, mutual decision which encompasses the reality of their conscience, reason and primary commitments. Their intimacy must be erotic instead of libidinous; their love must overflow from an abundance that desires communion, rather than an emptiness which needs to be filled up. Although such love may be difficult to maintain, I believe that the intensity of prayer and the strength of one's sense of commitment to spouse, community, other friends, or to one's ideal self are two essential factors which can keep sexual expression from becoming inordinate.

How does Gustafson's conception of celibate passion relate to friendship between women and men? Should the standards for physical expression within such friendship be as fluid as those she advocates for celibate passion? There is one obvious difference between intergender friendship and what I have called friendship and what she calls celibate passion: as I have characterized it, friendship seeks a balance that will keep the friends from falling in love; celibate passion appears, in contrast, to seek a balance that will allow those who have fallen in love to refrain from engaging in sexual intercourse.

Yet what she says about celibate passion could be relevant to intergender friendship. Not only can both sorts of connections between men and women have sexual undertones, but friends who lose their balance might find celibate passion a better place to land than full-blown adultery or fornication. Should, then, friends be "fully sensuous and spontaneously tactile"? Can they, permissibly or wisely, engage in erotic interactions that fall short of intercourse?

Gustafson's intention of avoiding rigidity and prudishness is laudable. In this area, as elsewhere, there is no simple algorithm for distinguishing imagination from rationalization and fiction-making. However, given human proneness toward fiction-making in this area, I would recommend considerably more caution toward physical affection than she seems to think necessary.

Four observations seem in order. First, friends who want to avoid having their friendship transformed into a romance (consummated or celibate) would do well to avoid physical expressions that they would not engage in with a sibling. What is relevant here is not whether going beyond this would be sinful, but whether it would be likely to push the balance within friendship from individuation toward union.

Second, few people will be able to engage in physical expressions to which their spouses, if they knew, would be likely to object without undermining what Haughey calls "presence" within their marriages. Third, while preserving a friendship is a challenge, this challenge pales beside trying to maintain what Gustafson seems to be recommending: a non-marital romance that is spontaneously tactile but not sexually inordinate. Finally, the degree of risk involved in spontaneous tactile expression would seem to vary proportionally with the intensity of the sexual undertones within a friendship. It is the friends who find their responses to one another least erotically charged who could most safely permit themselves the greatest liberty in this area. That may seem ironic; it also seems the wise dictate of a disciplined heart. Such discipline will not be easy; Gustafson's recommendation of intense prayer is surely applicable here. Grace will be needed both for achieving discipline and for repairing any lapses from it.

It is important to remember that in genuine befriending, whether same-gender or intergender, what is of central concern is the friend's fulfilling his or her destiny. Lewis claims that "it is the very mark of Eros that when he is in us we had rather share unhappiness with the Beloved than be happy on any other terms. . . . Eros never hesitates to say, 'Better this than parting. Better to be miserable with her than happy without her. Let our hearts break provided they break together.'"

If this is so, where one or both of the friends are married, there will be a natural braking system within any genuine friendship that encounters any gravitational pull toward eros caused by their genders. A friend may be able to say "I'd rather be miserable with her than happy without her," but as a friend he can never say "I'd rather she be miserable with me than happy without me." No one who takes his friend's good to heart could wish that she sacrifice her happiness or her integrity for his sake. If one finds himself willing to do so, he is not a friend and instead is engaging in fiction-making and rationalization.

Lewis points out that charity (neighbor love) should also control eros's reckless intemperance, and so it should. This, however, is different from the point I wish to make here, which is that the nature of friendship itself inhibits its transformation into eros. If friendship and romantic love are in part distinguished by their location on the continuum between union and individuation, there is likely to be a zone on that continuum where it is difficult to distinguish friendship (which may feel but creatively resist the sexual tension generated by recognizing the friend's excellences as a member of his or her gender) and romantic love (which may be restrained from its characteristic expression by charity). Here, there is importance in a name; our emotions are not under our instantaneous voluntary control, but they are shaped over time by the narratives we tell ourselves about them. That is why it is vital for friends, as part of the discipline of friendship, to speak the language of friendship, not of romance, to one another and to themselves in thought about one another.

Friends cannot be indifferent to the health of their friends' marriages without ceasing to be friends. If "the fire in the blood" threatens to overpower love's disciplined heart, genuine friendship should lead them to sacrifice the friendship for their friend's sake. Similar things can be said about situations in which nonsexual jealousy on the part of the friend's spouse makes the friendship a threat to the friend's marriage.

The creative relationship between vows, safe space and friendship is compellingly captured by Madeleine L'Engle in her poem "Lovers Apart" [to which the reader may wish to refer]. ❧

Untitled

Peter W. Gray

Your

words

are so

you and you are strong and

aware of other light

like a storm of white

blossoms or

the last petal

you know and have been

a-

round

the painful:

wonderfull is wonder - meant

again, you.

❧

Modern Friendship

Brian P. McGuire

CONTINUING INTEREST in friendship, but as a secular phenomenon, appears in the writings of the philosopher Montaigne (1533–92). His essay on friendship shows hesitation about the possibility of friendship in a world of intrigue and falsity. Like Petrarch, Montaigne cultivated his friends not as allies in a community network but as sharers of his solitude, comforters in time of need, and supporters in the solace of the intellectual life. His essay was written on the death of his best friend, whose loss he felt he never would get over or be able to compensate for. Montaigne remembered his Cicero in pointing out the uniqueness of friendship and its rarity in history, but he went further and made true friendship into an almost unattainable goal. In the twelfth century the Cistercians had looked upon friendship as available for any good monk, while in the sixteenth century it receded into the distance as a prize only for the highly learned and very sensitive man.

Here, as with the fourteenth-century humanists, Cicero was well known for his teaching on friendship but was hardly followed in his political dimension. For Montaigne friendship had nothing to do with the state, the community, or any common effort to change the conditions of society. It served as a refuge for the individual rather than as point of departure for involvement in any community. In writing of the devotion that Caius Blossius in ancient Rome had shown to Caius Gracchus, Montaigne recalled how Blossius had said that if Gracchus asked him to set fire to the temples of Rome, he would have obeyed him. Blossius would have done so because he was the friend of Gracchus:

They were friends before they were citizens, friends to one another before they were either friends or enemies to their country, or friends to ambition and revolt. Having absolutely given themselves up to one another, each had absolute control over the reins of the other's inclinations.

When friendship in this manner comes absolutely first, we have arrived at a modern practice emphasizing the passionate and individual element in friendship and have left behind the classical-medieval ideal that considered friendship a personal bond integrated into commitment to the good of the community. Montaigne's uncompromising view provides a foundation for the twentieth-century Cambridge writer E. M. Forster's perhaps better-known assertion that if he had to choose between betraying his friend or betraying his country, he hoped he would have the guts to betray his country! For Aristotle, Aelred, and Thomas Aquinas, such a choice would have seemed self-contradictory, for they insisted on friends being made and kept as part of involvement in a community. For classical-medieval writers, the two allegiances of friendship and community belonged together. For Montaigne, however, as for E. M. Forster, friendship became a supreme value that sometimes had to be chosen exclusively of all others. This radical isolation of friendship helps explain why Montaigne claimed that all earlier writings on friendship seemed cold and lifeless to him. In the face of his own emotions for his dead friend, "even the treatises which antiquity has left us on the subject seem flat to me in comparison with my own feeling." Montaigne's problem lay not only in his keen sense of loss but also in his view of friendship as an emotional involvement cut off from the world of rational choices in which the classical and medieval worlds had placed close human bonds.

In Montaigne friendship lost its place as a participant in the harmony and proportion of the good community in which friendship had been able to share in classical Rome and in twelfth-century monastic life. Montaigne, who in reality led an active life with political involvements, wrote about friendship as a lonely pursuit. He wanted to be a *homme de lettres* as Petrarch had been, commenting on the conditions of his time, writing poetry to his intimates, and harbouring boundless affection for one friend. In Montaigne we are only one step away from the nineteenth-century cult of romantic love which is at odds with a repressive social structure from which lovers have to flee.

When friendship becomes something attainable only for the few, when community is seen as either undesirable or all-encompassing, and when the salvation of the individual is seen in totally individual terms rather than in the context of a supportive community, we have left the classical-medieval synthesis and have entered the modern european world. In the modern separation of the loves of the individual from the life of the community, private and public life no longer connect. It becomes necessary to follow E. M. Forster and choose one loyalty rather than another.

The recent appearance and enthusiastic reception of the study *Habits of the Heart: Individualism and Commitment in American Life* shows a contemporary interest in how individuals affect their surroundings by their beliefs about themselves and their actions in terms of community. At the same time, modern monks, who see themselves more than ever as descendents not of seventeenth-century silence and enclosure but as heirs of twelfth-century affectivity, are seeking to open their way of life to young people for whom the experience of friendship is a necessary part of existence rather than something that has to be left behind in the world.

Looking back over the experiences and modes of expression that have characterized community and individual life and loves, we can return to the words of Anselm of Canterbury:

> Wherever you are being loved, you cannot be, but
> wherever you are, you can be loved and be good.

Anselm was writing to an unhappy monk at Canterbury who did not understand why he could not return to Bec to be with his friend Anselm, even though Anselm had claimed to love him greatly. Anselm's maxim was anchored in the teaching of the Rule of Saint Benedict on obedience and humility, as well as stability. These came first, but the structure they provided enabled a monk to participate in a community where love could be shown and where friendships were possible and even desirable. In this scheme social structure is not the enemy but the ally of human closeness. Since nineteenth-century romanticism, we have seen "society" as the culprit in the separation of human beings from each other. In Anselm's mind, the society of the monastery was precisely what was necessary for monks who were each other's friends to grow and develop in these friendships.

The isolation of personal friendship from community life that took place in the late medieval and early modern world has led since the nineteenth century to a denial of the social and political dimension in human bonds. Bernard of Clairvaux insisted on this dimension, and yet generations of students have asked how he possibly could have been a good abbot and yet have traversed Europe in order to influence events. Bernard's answer would have been that he owed it to his friends to use the power he had at his command: to spread the Order, to bring more monks into it, and to secure its position in the world of his day.

Monastic friendship may have been merely a peripheral cultural phenomenon that today is all but forgotten, despite increasing interest in the general subject of friendship. But the experience of Anselm, Aelred and Bernard, as well as that of the lesser figures in their vicinity, points out that the great divide in our culture comes not between classical and medieval worlds but between medieval and modern times. Thomas Aquinas could use the language of Aristotle in defining friendship. Aelred could turn to Cicero. But when the *Imitation of Christ* insisted that the saintly man give up his friend in the world in order to become a friend of God, the author was making a distinction that would have seemed unnecessary and even perverse to many twelfth-century monks. When Francis de Sales distinguished between friendships among the laity and particular friendships among the religious and warned against these, he replaced the medieval belief in personal bonds as part of community life by open suspicion of close friendships.

The writings of Thomas à Kempis and Francis de Sales may have only limited influence in our own day, but for centuries they provided ammunition for confessors, vocational directors, and school teachers. In this sombre world view, which could easily revive in the coming years, we are alone with God, hermits in the desert of modern life, even within

33

the religious community. Here we have come a long way from the twelfth-century synthesis which made the monastery into a paradise, a garden of friends, whose very existence provoked and transformed the world of which monastic community formed an integral part. ❧

chaste loving . . .
Mary Anne Huddleston

. . . enchantment
with the lotus blossoms
in the near lagoon,

. . . restraint
in garnering them.

❧

PART TWO

REALITIES

❧

Each friendship . . . [has] a certain rhythm.

—Susan Koppelman, *Women's Friendships*

A Time to Talk

Robert Frost

When a friend calls to me from the road
And slows his horse to a meaning walk,
I don't stand still and look around
On all the hills I haven't hoed,
And shout from where I am, "What is it?"
No, not as there is a time to talk.
I thrust my hoe in the mellow ground,
Blade-end up and five feet tall,
And plod: I go up to the stone wall
For a friendly visit.

❦

"Dear Henry"
Evelyn Waugh

Abingdon Arms,
Beckley,
Oxford.
[20 July 1929]

Dear Henry,

I was relieved to get your letter because once when I wrote a book a young man called Carew whom I had always liked wrote to tell me how good he thought my book was and I was so disgusted by his letter that I never could speak to him again without acute embarrassment and I thought perhaps my letter had had that effect on you well I am glad it hasn't.

I have written 25,000 words of a novel in ten days. It is rather like P. G. Wodehouse all about bright young people. I hope it will be finished by the end of the month & then I shall just have time to write another book before your party.

By the way would you like a seventeenth (or eighteenth I'm not sure) century water colour of the Prodigal Son which I bought in Malta for a wedding present or are you against "antiques" & would rather have a labour saving device for the kitchen?

Nancy Mitford came & drove us to Savernake on Sunday & I formed a clear impression that she & Robert are secretly married or is that my novelists imagination?

In the evenings I sit with the famous in the kitchen drinking beer. I like so much the way they don't mind not talking. Rich people always get shy when there's a silence or else they start thinking but in this public house they will all sit mute for five or ten minutes and then just go on talking at exactly the place where they left off. Were they like that at Birmingham. By the way *did* you say what the papers said you said about being jolly good pals with the boys at the works & all that? (I didn't know about Ld. Rosebery and was rather impressed.)

Do go and see Evelyn & Nancy. I've just sent them some caviar so you could eat that.

Are you going to Bryan & Diana's party I might go up for it if I thought there would be anyone who wouldn't be too much like the characters in my new book.

I know what you mean about purple patches. My new book is black with them—but then I live by my pen as they say and you don't.

Yours
Evelyn

My distinguished sentiments to your young lady. I hope she's still firm about Talkies

"My even more dearest friend"

Patricia Frazer Lamb

London, England
August 14, 1961

My even more dearest friend,

Alas, alas, it is all too quickly ended, and now how many more years will it be? Not one iota different are you, except maternal, wifely, womanly instead of girlish, loving instead of flirtatious, but the sparkle, the wit, the intelligence, the charm, all there, enhanced, I think, possibly, by your trials and tribulations over these years. They have left their mark indeed, but a good one; indeed a *hall*mark, one might say. It wasn't *long* enough, that chatter-filled week! It flashed by, leaving scraps of hazy memories of this and that conversation about this and that topic, but I am *so* happy to have been with you and shared your life, even for that brief instant.

But I must do my duty now (my bread-and-butter letter, as the English say)—many thanks for your hospitality to me that week, for putting up with my sermons and alarums. I do hope something has come up for Hans and that immediate future prospects seem less dismal. Write, write, and tell me how all goes.

Joyce, I don't know what I should say about all the things we talked of. I think nothing for the moment, as it is all still too fresh, and anyway, we said all the important things and know how the other feels about ourselves and marriage and children and art. The great thing is to go on elaborating and personalizing events and people and emotions. Here in England, Philip is terribly good about splitting our time equally with and away from the children. That is, while we're in London, he stays with them all day while I rush about shopping and gazing, and I stay home that night while he goes to a play or cinema, and the next day vice versa. We go out en masse (or rather, en messe) a couple of days a week and hire a baby-sitter two nights a week. It works very well. I love going places by myself anyway.

We had a grand reunion; the separation did us both a world of good, me especially! I think, anyway. I feel a great deal more settled and content, with P., with the children, with my lot and my chosen way of life. I have decided to give up my U.S. citizenship and to take out a British passport, but P. says wait until my U.S. one expires next year, then do it (he knows my rash ways so well). But I think I shall be unchanged then. London seems particularly lovely this summer. Is it the aching nostalgia of an aging beauty past her prime and effectiveness, her only power lying in the ability to stir men's memories of past glories and triumphs? I don't care. It is all such a slow process. I'd rather be in on the death of the Greek empire than the Roman one.

I must send you my article from the *Christian Science Monitor* of July 8th, smack dab in the middle of the editorial page, with a real live by-line! I'm frightfully proud, though probably I'll never get another published. They've even heightened it with a map of Africa, Tanganyika appropriately darkened, and a big picture of Mr. Nyerere, our Prime Minister. I have written another, on finance, and sent it off, and am working on a third, on women.

We think we have a house, for more than we had intended to pay, and a little larger—drawing room, dining room, study, kitchen, pantry, half-bath downstairs, four bedrooms and a bath up, three-quarter-acre garden (roses and fruit trees), and a couple of buildings that look as if they used to be a coach house, a garden shed, a coalbin. We have paid a 10% deposit and now just sit back and wait for our lawyer to do the rest. It will probably still be another three to four weeks before we can move in. We'll have to get a seven-year mortgage on it, and hope to God we can rent it furnished while we are in Africa, at an exorbitant rent, or we'll never be able to meet the payments. That shouldn't be too hard though, to rent it, if we can manage to scrape enough secondhand furniture together to fill the place.

Our nearest village is in a posh area, and we're surrounded by big estates, we in our little Victorian villa (villa being a condescending term in England, not at all the American idea of Mediterranean grandeur). It's a very lovely, settled, English area, rolling green wooded countryside of the Sussex downs, farms, the two nearest villages both ancient and tiny, but Hastings, from which we are about three miles inland, a not very prepossessing seaside town on the Channel. We are about an hour and a half by train from London, so we shan't be able to rent the house to commuters, which was our original plan, but it is such a good area, everyone assures us we shan't have any trouble leasing it out. It is about a hundred years old, brick, with big bay windows in front; it is set back from the road by an enormous hedge and wide lawn, and has a little road alongside the house, entered by big double gates.

We are pleased with it and hope we can move in by the 12th of September, when our five weeks in our present flat are up. We rented a two-bedroomed flat in London from a woman who went to France for five weeks, and must be out by the day she returns. It's terribly difficult to find any kind of furnished accommodation that will take children (in fact, lots of the estate agents who do rentals have signs in their windows saying, "No pets, children, or coloureds"—ugh, on all three counts). Before we moved in here last week, we stayed in a sandy little four-berth trailer on the south coast for a week!

I must say, it's tremendous fun looking at land and houses that might actually be one's own with the flick of a pen. It makes one feel rather omnipotent and regal. I think we shall be very happy with our East Sussex house, if it all goes through. The old ladies who own it now have a piano in the dining room which we have offered 10 pounds for (it's an awful old thing, but—a piano), and they've accepted, so although we owe thousands, we possess two pianos. I told you I've bought a *good* tropicalized studio piano from a friend in Tanganyika for 85 pounds and am picking it up in December when we return and pass through Dar es Salaam. The old crock here we shall just leave in the house, to be played or not by the tenants, as they wish.

I wish we could furnish it to suit ourselves, but cheapness and utility will have to be the prime considerations for absolutely everything from kitchen cupboards to beds and sofas, all secondhand from ads and sales and auction rooms—carpets too. But the great thing is that it will be ours, ours, ours. A neighbor informed Philip that the soil is so fertile, a previous owner had actually supported himself market-gardening on the 3/4 acre! I feel a real land hunger suddenly.

The children are loving England and are wonderfully responsive tourists, especially Christopher, who adores the policemen on horseback, the escalators in the shops, the underground, electricity! They are very good about new baby-sitters in the evenings and being dragged all over the place by car, foot and bus. Christopher, alas, seems to have forgotten all his hard-learned letters and numbers.

We are madly looking for old battered furniture with which to fill our eight-roomed house, and have been having fair luck. We've spent about $45.00 so far, and have quite a lot of stuff—a double and a single bed, a desk, two leather armchairs ($2 each!), a kitchen table, two dining room chairs, a chest of drawers, a couple of cabinets, a big kerosene heater. England is amazingly cheap for this sort of thing, even antiques are very inexpensive.

I must end, and egg and bread the tots. My dearest Joyce, it is as if all the years had never been. You must write right away and tell me about jobs and homes.

> Much, much dearest love,
> Pat

"My dear, dear friend"
Kathryn Joyce Hohlwein

Columbus, Ohio
August 29, 1961

My dear, dear friend,

I broke into tears upon receiving and reading this first letter of yours since your departure, this inaugurating letter of a whole new series of years, probably—certainly of experiences. And only a letter from you, I believe, or Hans, could do this to me. Increasingly I think that I should feel crushed if for one reason or another our correspondence should cease or become dilute and ineffectual.

I had been about to write you, and would probably have written you a sorrowing if not peevish letter, for I, and we both, were very eager to hear from you, to know that you crossed the Atlantic without broken eardrums, that Christopher delighted in your bright reunion, that Philip was grateful to have you back. But I had to wait to hear from you first. I hadn't your address, and now rather than send off my petulance, I must utter huzzahs and pride in your success with the *Monitor* article. You cannot guess how it pleases me—or perhaps you can, for I know you would take equal delight if ever I should have my attempts printed in such a first-rate publication. Is Philip as pleased as he should be? Good journalism is not an easy art, and a great many things can be put in that way only.

Your departure left a vacuum in my life from which I suffered as if from withdrawal symptoms. I felt great irritation in the brevity of the visit, and a certain gnawing restiveness, if not envy—which I know you marked, but which I have since come to acknowledge as unrealistic and unproductive, at least in its concentration upon detail. In any case, I have since adjusted to the fact and the truth that our respective lives naturally dictate differing possibilities, choices and chances, and it is foolish of me to yearn for things in the context of your European, your British-dominated mode.

The day after you left Milwaukee, Hans received a long-distance call from the chairman of the enormous and highly reputed Art Department of Ohio State University, announcing that Hans had been selected from twenty candidates to become appointed as an instructor at the university. We were both delighted (again, you must acknowledge the scope of our choices), for this is a real academic step forward, even though Columbus is sort of nowhere on earth, and Hans has already termed it the "green hell of Ohio"—denoting primarily the climate, but perhaps the environment as well. The salary isn't good, the loss of rank is a little discouraging, but these demerits are more than compensated for by the fact that he has been accepted by one of the big ten universities, to teach in an art department (almost unparalleled) in an American university, and to teach a specialty of his, drawing and studio applied appreciation, two courses which will beautifully concentrate and channel his gifts and natural emphases. Who knows how long we will be here? Assuredly until he has proven himself in the task, probably until he receives tenure, and possibly even longer.

Furthermore (you'll consider this as mad), Hans bought us a house here on a trip to Columbus only shortly after you left. The down payment was only $500, astonishingly minimal, and the house itself, in excellent repair, only $14,000—staggering to you, but low in American terms. We are already rather firmly ensconced, and I am delighting in the privacy, the space, the garden, and the dead-end street, which frees me from, say, three-quarters of the agony I feel each time I hear screeching brakes. All our propertied friends assure us that Hans did an economically sane thing in the purchase, for in America at least, where real estate over the past decades has been the steadiest and most certain of almost all equity, anyone with a sensible eye to home improvement, and a willingness and capacity to keep a house up (are you lifting your eyebrows at this point?), can scarcely lose money, and in fact stands almost certainly to profit. Hence, if we leave Ohio after only three years, we will at least regain the rent we have paid, having had in the meantime the pleasure of living in our own sphere, and since we intend to redo the bathroom, we stand to gain perhaps $1000. If all goes well, and if I follow your good tips as I intend to (submerging my will, as you say), we shall hope to pay off the mortgage within five years, and have the full equity to work with.

The house itself? A two-story, three-bedroomed house, with a large living room, a dining room separated by French doors, a most pleasant and workable kitchen, and a quite splendid basement which Hans will use as studio. It's by no means the ordinary basement, for the previous owner had converted it into a workshop for his photography studio. Thus there are fine overhead lights quite ideal for a painter, second or third only to a skylight, and he has ample space there, besides being quite removed from the confusion of family and childhood activity. The house is white shingle, very Midwestern and architecturally not at all distinctive, but very clean and in its way attractive, with its newly painted green shutters, wide porch, and lawn front and back. We've a lovely little maple tree in front, a sprawling apple tree in back, and a back garden, albeit unkempt and weed-ridden, which slopes down to an alley through varying stages of petunias, sweet peas, lettuce, rhubarb, marigolds, carrots, hollyhocks, roses and a brick path. We both find the possibilities are sufficiently circumscribed, particularly by the tight squeeze the adjacent houses put on ours, that it is quite impossible to conceive of this house as our ultimate one, or to conceive of it with quite the sense of futurity that you do yours. But it is rather nicely coincidental that we all became house-owners at about the same time, I feel. And please, by the way, NEVER assume that the details of your life bore me. Always assume that they interest me profoundly, as they do.

The neighborhood is not posh, as yours evidently is, but merely steady, peopled with solid, pin-curled, middle-aged, middle-class women. Goodness, how I dislike middle-class America—I feel utterly, utterly alien from it, and cannot but regard its children almost as monsters. This feeling comes and goes, but at times is quite insupportable.

I worry that Philip did not like Hans's prints. You needn't exude reassurances, but I do hope he will want them to be hanging somewhere in your new home, which is likely to be where, by the way? I do want to know where you will be at Christmas, for I have some little things to send.

This letter does go on and on—there are and I presume always will be so many endless things to comment on, as now. The ghastly world tension, the damnable bomb shelters we are urged to build in our backyards—how seriously should a responsible person take these things? I am bursting with affection for you, with pride in our friendship.

Love,
Joyce

To a Poet
Eleanor Fitzgibbons

Tongue-tied by joy
I listen to you
reading your poems
and bringing me
to life in them.

You cannot see

the bright phoenix from its ashes rising
on the dark skies
of my silence

or the flowers
opening in the rain
on my desert sands.

❦

Companions on the Way
Shirley du Boulay

The Anglican philosopher and novelist C. S. Lewis and the Benedictine monk Bede Griffiths each brought spiritual growth to countless people. What is less known is how they helped each other. Shirley du Boulay, a biographer of Bede Griffiths, charts their unusual friendship.

BEDE GRIFFITHS WAS, above all, a contemplative, a man who needed solitude. He was also reserved, restrained and, until late in his life, a man who repressed his emotions. As a young man he was typical of the Edwardian England into which he was born, a time when the "stiff upper lip" was admired, when emotions were to be repressed, not shared.

But a love of solitude is not incompatible with a capacity for friendship—in fact it could be argued that those with the greatest gift for friendship are those who can best tolerate, indeed enjoy, their own company. Nor need a reserved temperament stand in the way of friendship.

Bede also had the advantage of being outstandingly good-looking, highly intelligent and a man of great charm and courtesy, who had no difficulty in relating to people, indeed who won the hearts of all who met him. Friendship was always of deep importance to him, but when he was a young man his relationships were not always as easy as those who knew him in later life might have expected.

One of the most significant friendships of his early life was with C. S. Lewis, who became his tutor at Oxford in 1927 when Bede changed from reading Classics to English Literature.

Lewis was only eight years his senior and had become a Fellow of Magdalen the year Bede came up. They immediately got on marvellously well together, the tutorial relationship soon ripening into a friendship so close that Bede wrote that it was through Lewis that he discovered the meaning of friendship.

Their relationship always had an element of the adversarial about it. At their very first meeting Bede explained how his wish to change from the Classics to English lay in the fact that he had lost faith in reason and the intellect and that Lewis could not possibly convince him to the contrary, as he was not open to reason on the subject. He wrote later that a tutorial with Lewis was a battle of wits and that it was through opposition that one came to friendship with him; Lewis himself said that their friendship began in disagreement and matured in argument. So they argued with the utmost freedom, in the way only those who are basically in tune with each other can argue.

Bede claimed not to understand why Lewis liked him, but the fact that he had met a worthy opponent must have had something to do with it. Lewis had not at that stage achieved the fame that was to be his and though Bede found him formidable and unshakeable, like many intelligent undergraduates he was not going to be cowed into instant submission and pursued his crusades, for instance against Dryden and Pope and the Age of Reason, which stood for all he despised, with a tireless fervour. Lewis found Bede one of the more intractable of his pupils, turning implied criticism into compliment by admitting that he was "one of the toughest dialecticians of my acquaintance." Bede admitted to being "surprised and rather pleased" by this.

Neither of them was Christian at the time. Indeed, Bede felt Christianity had ceased to have any significance for the present day, arguing that a new religion was needed and that its prophets were Wordsworth, Shelley and Keats. His religion was the worship of nature and he could see no connection between the God manifested in nature and the God preached in church.

At first their relationship was about the way Lewis taught his pupil and influenced his reading, but soon it became the story of their shared search for faith. More and more, they began to appreciate the religious background to the English literature they read, what they called "this Christian mythology," and the idea that it might be true began to dawn on them. By the time Bede left Oxford in 1929 they had been converted to theism, Lewis encapsulating this stage of their friendship, rather curiously using the third person, by saying: "Both now believed in God, and were ready to hear more of him from any source, pagan or Christian."

They became Christians at almost the same time, Lewis dating the moment precisely to the Trinity term of 1929 and saying it was "chiefly by reason," though Bede wrote that "both he and I came to religion by way of literature." Whatever Bede's feelings about reason, there was probably truth in both explanations. They felt they were taking part in a Christian Renaissance, and both men published accounts of their conversions in the mid-1950s, Lewis dedicating his autobiography, *Surprised by Joy*, to Bede, whom he describes as his "chief companion on this stage of the road."

After Bede left Oxford the two men corresponded regularly, and though, unfortunately, Bede's letters are no longer extant, more than 40 of Lewis's shed light on the way the relationship developed. They wrote mostly in affection, though sometimes a note of irritation creeps in, for after Bede became a Roman Catholic he expressed the enthusiasm of the convert, hailing a new discovery he expected his friend to share. But Lewis was embarrassed by this enthusiasm and did not wish to discuss their differences. An Ulsterman and a Protestant to his bones, he felt that Bede was trying to convert him to Catholicism and put his cards on the table soon after Bede had become a Benedictine. He wrote:

> I had better say once and for all that I do not intend to discuss with you in the future, if I can help it, any of the questions at issue between our respective Churches. . . . I could not, now you are a monk, use that freedom in attacking your position which you undoubtedly would use in attacking mine.

Lewis was one of the first people to visit Bede when he was a young monk at Prinknash Abbey, and it seems that some disagreement surfaced then, for on his return to Oxford Lewis wrote, on Boxing Day 1934, assuring Bede that he had no need to apologise, for their friendship was beyond any sort of danger:

> If I object at all to what you said, I object not as a friend or as a guest, but as a logician. If you are going to argue with me on the points at issue between our Churches, it is obvious that you must argue to the truth of your position not from it. The opposite procedure only wastes your time and leaves me to reply, moved solely by embarrassment: "*Tu sei santo ma tu no sei filisofo!*" ("You may be holy but you're no philosopher!").

But Bede would not let the subject go, on one occasion writing: "You have no reason to fear that anything you say can have any serious effect on me."

Lewis responded with asperity (20 February 1936):

> The underlying assumption that anyone who knew you would feel such a fear is not only funny but excruciatingly funny...ask the Prior if he sees the joke: I rather think he will.... You, in your charity, are anxious to convert me: but I am not in the least anxious to convert you. You think my specifically Protestant beliefs a tissue of damnable errors: I think your specifically Catholic beliefs a mass of comparatively harmless human tradition which may be fatal to certain souls under special conditions, but which I think suitable for you!

Bede was, the letter claimed, only interested in differences—in any case Lewis had no wish to debate with a man who began by saying no argument could possibly move him.

Lewis later apologised for being somewhat ill-tempered when he wrote this letter, which had riled Bede enough for him to recall it years later, when he admitted that his enthusiasm had been excessive and explained that he had no wish to convert Lewis to Catholicism, but simply that he enjoyed the debate and wanted it to continue.

With only one side of the correspondence extant, Bede's contributions can only be surmised from Lewis's references, but it is clear that the two men sent each other their latest articles and books, giving appreciative though always outspoken reactions, and that the relationship between tutor and pupil had developed into one between equals.

Yet no account of their friendship would be true if it did not admit that there were many areas in which they were far apart. Bede felt that Lewis was fundamentally conservative, one of the great defenders of the European cultural tradition—indeed Lewis described himself as "a dinosaur"; Bede, though steeped in traditional values, was essentially radical, concerned to find a new vision for the twentieth century.

Lewis claimed not to attempt "the precipices of mysticism"; for Bede the experience of union with God was the goal of man's life on earth. Most of all they disagreed about the importance of the Church. Lewis had little interest in the Fathers; for Bede they were the bedrock of Western monasticism.

Lewis was quite unconcerned about the Church as an institution, holding to "mere Christianity," which he believed was common to all committed Christians from the followers of the Salvation Army to Roman Catholics, and considering religion "a matter of good men praying alone, and meeting by twos and threes to talk of spiritual matters."

Though Bede was to become very critical of it, the question of the Church was all-important to him, indeed it was the concept of the Church as the Mystical Body of Christ which had led him to embrace the Roman Catholic faith.

Bede never wished to exaggerate the differences between them, and felt that what they shared grew rather than diminished as the years rolled by; certainly their disagreements never shook their friendship. Despite Bede's going to India in 1955 the two men never lost touch and at their last meeting, just a month before Lewis's death in 1963, Lewis reminded Bede that they had been friends for nearly 40 years. Looking back over these years Bede wrote of his debt to Lewis's critical mind and his kindness: "There are not many things in my life more important than that friendship." 🌿

Memories of Teilhard

Pierre Leroy, S.J.

THIS IMAGE, ENGRAVED IN MY MEMORY over fifty years ago, is as clear today as it ever was. Why, I cannot say. It is something I fail to understand since the picture is quite an ordinary one.

It happened in Peking where I had just moved. I was living with Pierre Teilhard, a fellow Jesuit and colleague. We were alone in the new institute of geo-biology and our fraternal relations were fast turning to friendship. I was under the impression that we had no secrets from each other.

One day, as I was going to the French hospital in Legations Road, I saw to my surprise a couple coming towards me—a man and a woman walking side by side in silent thought. It was Teilhard and an American lady whom he had mentioned to me. She was about the same age as he, a striking figure, though quiet in her bearing and dignified in the simplicity of her dress. It is this picture that remains in my mind.

I learned later that this American was Lucile Swan and that she was living opposite us in the same street. Her European style house was graced with a garden where I was to meet her several times. This was in 1940. Teilhard was to be found there often also, translating some of his articles into English. We all used to have tea together.

She was a sculptress and had modeled a face for the "Peking Man," an old fossil skull studied by Weidenreich at the Peking Union Medical College. This successful work had won her recognition in scientific circles. The bust was christened "Nelly" by us privately.

The pressure put on the Americans living in Peking by the Japanese army prompted a number of them to return to

America. In 1941, Lucile made the wise decision to join them and departed in late August.

Letters made up for the absence and the distance. The value of the resulting correspondence between the two friends is left to the appreciation of the reader. In fact, it brought them together again, for the beginning of their friendship face to face had been somewhat strained. Lucile saw a contradiction between the evolutionary theories of Teilhard and his practice of chastity. "You admit the necessity of working thought out and with material in order to reach ideas abstract or God-like, but you deny the use of material (human) in order to reach the abstract or the God-like. You will say you deny only one part of human love but I think you are evading the question, for the physical is not only a very important but an essential part for the race."

Lucile was not mistaken: it is quite natural for the physical act to play its part in the manifestation of human love.

Neither was Teilhard wrong for he was fully aware of the power of "the feminine," that force of attraction towards union, not only among human beings but for the whole universe. His conception of union between a man and a woman went far beyond physical union. Some men and women are called individually to live the love of God in a different way. By denying themselves certain material pleasure, they seek strongly to give themselves totally to a loving God. Teilhard was one such person and everyone knows that he remained faithful until his death.

Lucile was not incapable of realizing the true value of her friend nevertheless. "What you are doing and what you have to offer is the most important thing in the world today."

* * *

Teilhard left Peking at the end of March 1946. He settled in his room on the Rue Monsieur in Paris with the firm intention of resuming the scholarly activities he had been pursuing before his [disciplinary] exile to China in 1926. An unexpected obstacle was to thwart his projects however. During the month of June 1947, he had a severe heart attack and, since his condition required extended hospital treatment, he entered a nursing home in the Rue Oudinot. I visited him frequently to see how he was getting on.

Meanwhile Lucile had arrived in Paris from America. She was staying in the Auteuil district and had let Teilhard know she would be coming to see him. The appointment came at the wrong moment; he was unfortunately otherwise engaged.

Lucile discovered with bitterness that her friendship had been superseded. The new friend was Rhoda, the former wife of Professor Hellmut de Terra, a scientist whose acquaintance Teilhard had made in Burma.

Teilhard was anxious that his two friends should not meet. And to me was entrusted the job of explaining the situation to Lucile. She was extremely vexed, but with time, things settled down again.

* * *

Teilhard's influence on Lucile did not have the effect that might have been expected. Intelligent and independent, she went on to follow a swami in Vedanta contemplation. Here is what Teilhard wrote to me on the matter: "Lucile has found peace of mind in a group directed by a Swami. In such circles spirituality seems to me to be terribly vague. But is it not the only issue for countless people who do not manage to pierce that formidable, hardened, outer shell that theologians qualify by the name of orthodoxy?"

Teilhard returned to America for the last time in the autumn of 1954. There in New York he found the ever-faithful Lucile. He died on the evening of Easter Sunday 1955 while talking with other guests who were also visiting at the New York home of Rhoda de Terra. ❧

"Lucile, dearest"
Pierre Teilhard de Chardin

Peking, 8 août, 1941.

Lucile, dearest,

I scarcely can realize that you are leaving today. And I still less realize that tomorrow Peking will be for me without you. But I want you to know that, above any sense of loneliness, I will feel stronger, in all directions, than when we landed here two years ago.—These two precious years of constant presence and uninterrupted mutual confidence have certainly achieved and sealed our friendship. This friendship is now strong enough to face everything, and to grow through.—As I told you these last days, I think that our dominant disposition has to be a stubborn and loving "confiance" in the Future. New experience and new environment are a universal condition of progress.—Thanks to you, I see more definitely what I believe, and what I have to fight for. I am convinced that your going to America is just a providential and necessary step in the constructive convergency of our lives. Go ahead in full peace, joy and hope.

Herewith I enclose a copy of the only "pious" object left, since years, on my working table. Hope you will not think it too much "roman catholic." For me this quite simple illustration is a vague representation of the universal "foyer" of attraction which we are aiming for. In this atmosphere we can always love each other more and better.————

Ever yours (et au *revoir*)!
P. T.

[The "pious" object was a postcard-size picture of the Sacred Heart of Jesus that Teilhard had brought from his home in the Auvergne.]

🌿

"Lucile dear"
Pierre Teilhard de Chardin

Institut de Géo-Biologie / Rue Labrousse / Peking, August 11, 1941

Lucile dear,

May these few lines reach Shanghai before you leave China, to bring you something of the deep of my heart! God bless you again and again for what you gave me since twelve years, and more specially during these last months!—And may we be together again—very soon.—

Here, I am still a little "ahuri" [bewildered] to be without you. Fortunately, I have been quite nicely entertained by friends, during these two days. After you left, Friday, Tillie and Eleanor took me with them for tea. On Saturday evening, I went to Raphaël. And yesterday I had lunch with the d'Anjou at Pao Ma Chang (Mme d'Anjou invited me, when you left, on the platform; she is certainly a sweet person).—I went to Pao Ma Chang in the Houghton's car. The whole d'Anjou family was there; they are so fond of each other that one forgets, or even likes, in them everything.—Today, the week begins without you. I do not mind any more to see the days passing too fast, now.—Just now I have to go to Vetch for the question of publications. Such a luck to have them to keep me busy!—As soon as the rush is over, I am decided to begin "L'atomisme de l'Esprit."—The "egg" is ripe by now, I think.—To write it will [make] me feel closer to you.

> Be happy—dearest—
> Everything is all right,—but I miss you.
> P. T.
> P. S. - Address your letters as before to the
> *PUMC (anatomy)*

Untitled
Emily Dickinson

Elysium is as far as to
The very nearest Room
If in that Room a Friend await
Felicity or Doom—

What fortitude the Soul contains,
That it can so endure
The accent of a coming Foot—
The opening of a Door—

❦

An Unsolved Mystery
Joyce Carol Oates

AN UNSOLVED MYSTERY is a thorn in the heart.

Many years after my friend Barbara's death I still think of
her with a stir of hope and dread. As if she hasn't died, yet. As
if there might be something I could do to prevent her dying.

We were eighteen years old, the final time we spoke on the
telephone. It has been that long.

I can't claim that I was Barbara's best friend in high
school—Barbara wasn't the type to have a "best" friend. But
we saw each other often and, for each, the other was the measure of sincerity: the opinion that mattered. We did not flat-

ter each other, nor did we withhold praise out of envy. Sometimes I wondered if Barbara, with her quick, frequently sharp tongue, was capable of lying.

Since Barbara lived in town, in an attractive residential neighborhood, and I lived twelve miles from town, I was sometimes invited to stay overnight at her house—which suggests, in retrospect, that we were close and might have shared secrets. In fact these overnight visits were rather formal. Mainly, Barbara and I did our schoolwork. Being earnestly, indefatigably "bright" students, we invariably did more than our teachers required of us. Amid classmates aggressively mature for their ages, the girls in particular (in those years girls *hoped* to become engaged directly out of high school, as a way of being shielded from seeking a "career"), we were anomalies: intellectually advanced for our ages, yet clearly young, immature, in other respects.

Barbara was large-boned, not fat, nor even plump, but thick-bodied; with a pale, smudged complexion; close-cropped, unstyled hair; a weak-muscled left eye of the kind called "wandering." It was the right eye that engaged you. She was shy, yet aggressive; seemingly withdrawn, yet capable of surprising, and wounding, with a sudden sarcastic or cynical remark, as if resentment built up powerfully in her, awaiting discharge. Because of my teenaged appearance—diminutive, dark, watchful—I was perceived as shy, though in fact I was not shy; yet I lacked Barbara's outspokenness. Even in self-defense I was incapable of a razor-swift, cutting remark.

We did not resemble each other physically at all. Yet in some mysterious way we were like sisters. Or twins.

I recall several occasions when, to my bewilderment, I was confused with Barbara, or Barbara with me. Once, swimming in the school pool, myopic and blinking, and hearing the teacher call out, "Barbara?—I mean, Joyce." Another time, overhearing a mutual friend say, "It *was* Joyce, wasn't it?—or, no, Barbara."

Barbara was scientific-minded, and competed successfully with the most favored boys in our class. I was literary-minded, a tireless reader. Yet we shared each other's interests and obsessions, to a degree. When I became caught up in reading American plays, especially the long, somber tragedies of Eugene O'Neill, Barbara read the plays, too, and my own awkward attempts at writing "tragedy." In turn, I read through *Scientific American* (to which Barbara had a subscription) and I accompanied Barbara to special exhibits at the natural history museum and the planetarium. In spring of our senior year, Barbara was awarded a scholarship to Cornell University, where she intended to study chemistry; I was awarded a scholarship to Syracuse University, where I intended to study comparative literature. So close were the Cornell and Syracuse campuses, it seemed certain we *must* see each other often.

Yet, for some reason, our friendship began to dissolve almost immediately, as soon as we left for college.

Barbara was a poor correspondent. If I wrote her three or four letters, she might be prodded into writing me one. Her letters were brief and apathetic; she mentioned several times the size of the Cornell campus—it was "unreal" and it was "strange." After Christmas break, Barbara stopped writing altogether. I telephoned once, in February, and was hurt by her affected coolness. "*Who*—?" she asked. As if she hadn't recognized my voice. Half-accusingly she said, "You sound different, somehow."

Not just why Barbara took her own life, in May of that year, but how—this is part of the mystery, for me. Sleeping pills, slashed wrists, poison?—I never knew, and never wanted to know. (Of course there were rumors, the most convincing being that Barbara had swallowed a corrosive chemical taken from a university laboratory.) Barbara's stunned, grieving parents spoke to no one outside the family about their tragedy. In those days it seemed reasonable to keep private facts private.

Yet memories of Barbara missing from my life actually predate her death. Why this is I don't know.

At Thanksgiving, a mutual girlfriend invited a number of us over for an impromptu party, and I was to pick up Barbara; but, when I arrived at her house, she'd changed her mind, greeting me wanly, unsmiling—"You go on without me, nobody's going to miss me." She had a migraine headache, she said. Her eyes did look swollen, reddened.

I tried to talk her into coming with me but she was stubborn, sullen. Standing in her old bathrobe regarding me with something like amusement. "Go on, go alone. Nobody is going to miss *me*."

So I went to our friend's house by myself and, it's true, no one exactly *missed* Barbara, as she'd predicted. This fact made a strong impression on me, in retrospect. *Don't die willfully, you won't be missed.* Yet, that evening, there was a sense of my being somehow incomplete, as if lacking someone—something? At one point a girl asked, unthinking, "Oh where's Joyce?—I mean Barbara," and everyone laughed; I joined in the laughter though feeling suddenly very strange, as if about to burst into tears. 🖋

Lenten Learning
Mary Anne Huddleston

Lord, it has been Lent
a long, long time this year.
Seventeen months before Ash Wednesday
it began, began with a concealment by a man,
no Judas this time, but a Jonathan.
And it and its daughter incidents,
so casual to him and to the passersby,
still gnaw into the marrow,
and the very midst of me.

Yes. It has been Lent
a long, long time this year.
But long Lents simplify.
And now I see, the Passion came to this:
who seemed to be His friends
preferred Him not.

❦

The Friend
Raymond Roseliep

We drove until the maples pointed how
the river was an autumn older too.

We stood beside the river:

                        not as boys
but men who looked for answers to the love
that neither had. He talked about the gulls,
stone faced and hungry, and although I felt
his want, I could not give even a child's
attachment to his need.

                    I dived into
my soul, disturbing relics of those others
who had swum when friendship was a word
like god

                (for then my christ was Midas who
                could make the spirit gold, and I had
                  welcomed
                brilliance till I burned with it and
                  learned
                the trick of drowning shadow from
                  that reach);

and there I kicked the almost emptiness
and licked at dark. I left my soul

and ran

a reel of river past his eye and said:
The water is a friendly place, but notice
how the slender gull dips gracefully
to touch a surface he will never probe.

The picture hurt his eye, and he seemed fearful
that the symbols would explode before
the riddle of my hand.

I shook my keys.
And he was ready to be driven back
to ordinary rounds and search the oldest
corners of our towns from end to end,
having found a little less than friend.

❦

For a Proud Friend Humbled

Jessica Powers

In that least place to which all mercies come
I find you now, settled in peace, at home,
poor little one of Yahweh. On your face
only response of love lies, with no trace
or drifting hint of what had brought you low.
Down steps of like unworthiness I go
weighted with heart (and how heart can oppress!)
to see you humbled into gentleness
(and into innocence) so utterly.
Pray me, my blessed, into your company.

Friday, June 1st
May Sarton

AT LAST A SHINING DAY that looks as though it would stay, not darken into a shower for a change. I have the morning for myself before Martha and Marita start filming, a little unexpected gift of time in which to sort things out. The day before yesterday as I read the *Times* I came upon Marynia Farnham's obituary. It is a blessing to know that she has been allowed to go at last, after these last years when she did not recognize anyone, talked only to herself in a strange singing monotone, the words incomprehensible. Now the long decline can be forgotten and the rich snowy days can come back when I used to drive over to Winchester to drink champagne in her great room filled with works of art, listen to music, and talk. The real Marynia can come back into memory, her flashing dark eyes, her laughter, and her salty wisdom.

I had been very lonely in Nelson when I first met her, and I shall never forget walking into that big room the first time . . . I felt I had come home at last. This was after I had been her patient and we had begun to be friends. She seemed, with her whippets around her, like some lady in a tapestry. Unbelievable in the midst of the cultural poverty with which I was surrounded to be in the presence again of such a civilized life and ethos! Not since Edith Kennedy, who had been dead thirty years or more then, had I found a person with whom I could talk about everything in depth, and who could bring to our exchanges such a wide frame of reference. In that room I learned a great deal. For her I wrote many poems, a whole book that has never been published. Let me place two of them here, in memoriam. ❦

A Birthday

This is a house inhabited
By Beatrix Potter, Mozart,
Gaston Lachaise,
A doll who offers a bunch of flowers
To the slow tinkle of a music box,
Two stuffed owls,
An old French clock—
A house full of good spells,
A house full of love,
Old and new,
Strange and simple,
Violent and merry.

And here in this magic house
Lives a passionate child
With great dark eyes,
A child who is also
A woman in her seventh decade,
A doctor of the human soul.

Three whippets and a white cat
Sleep on her bed.
Marynia wakes early
For fear of missing something—

Light on a single yellow leaf,
A scarlet tanager at the feeder,
Once a newborn donkey
Standing beside its mother.
Who knows what may happen
Early in the morning?

Marynia wakes
Before the telephone
Brings its weeping voices
Into the house.
One hand, large and gentle,
Strokes a dog's head
While she summons her wisdom,
Cuts woe down
With luminous reason,
Demands courage.

It has needed massive powers
Of light and compassion
To be so ready for instant response
Early in the morning
Or late at night.
But "I am always expecting a surprise,"
Marynia says.

She gets impatient
When nothing happens—
Better a cat up a tree
Than nothing at all.

"And what next?" Marynia asks,
"What's going to happen next?"

Right now
Hunca Munca is coming in with the cake.
Blow out the candles and make a wish.
That's what happens next.

"And after that?"
A journey, a book to write,
A new year, and always love,
Love knocking at the door.
Peter Rabbit tore his jacket
And will be very late.
Aunt Jemima could not get up the hill.

But we, some owls, a bear, and a bee,
We are here, you see,
To say, "Happy Birthday!
Happy New Year, Marynia!"
With hoots, hugs, and honey,
With love and ceremony.

The Place beyond Action

In these airy balances
Between music and poetry
Between kinds of love
And kinds of deprivation,
How softly we must tread!
Of course you, secret person,
Learned long ago to walk the tightrope
Between attachment and detachment,
Learned never to stumble
On its perilous tension . . .

Nevertheless,
Attentive to a whisper,
I know your passion
And feel your violence.

Sometimes I love the somber person
Who rises up from a glass of wine
To curse the "cultural desert"
Where we both live,
God knows why.

Sometimes I hate the somber person
Who makes me feel like a desert
Where nothing can bloom,
For I am the prisoner
Of what I see
And can do nothing to change.

You are alone and should not be,
Rich Ceres, great giver,
That is the truth,
And it is hardly to be borne.
I bear it with an ill grace,
Trying to remember
Your valor, resilience,
The fertile mind,
The changing moods
Like clouds over a landscape
Of hills and lakes, light-shot,
Never at rest, expecting surprises.

In the airy balance
Where we sometimes achieve communion
It will always be possible
To move outside the deprivations,
Yours and mine,

Into a curious detached region
Natural to you, achieved by me,
That is music, that is poetry.
It is the place beyond action
And even sometimes beyond thought—
At worst unnatural
So much must be denied,
At best, nourishing,
So much has been accepted.

❦

IT ALL ENDED BADLY, because of senility, but what does that matter now? Now I can come back to the essence, and the essence was life-giving, and remains so.

While one stops to mourn the dead and to reapprehend their reality, life keeps bringing its new relations and marvelous passages where we witness growth in each other. The day I saw the obit in the *Times*, Jill Felman, my young writer friend, came to tea. For the past five years we have met at long intervals to revel in a long intimate dialogue about our work and our lives. I have watched Jill grow—she is twenty-five now I think. She is breaking through her Jewish heritage that seemed for a time both her richest source as a writer, and at the same time, a prison. She is breaking through into her real life as a caring woman who will probably not marry. I saw that in her and she saw in me at once, she said, some ease, some absence of tension, a recovery. I was surprised that she saw it so quickly... surprised and pleased. Jill is off to Israel for eleven weeks, excited on the edge of adventure, on the edge of doing good work.

Yesterday I got a haunting record of Japanese music for flute and harpsichord, with a letter in it from the Phoenix ... so I call Dorothy Koeberlin who is battling increasing disability as a diabetic. Through letters I have known her for years, always refreshed and given courage by her courage, her acute sense of life as it is more and more taken from her. In this letter she says,

> I had three transfusions but am still unable to walk, and oh, how I long for that. I can remember hot muggy days in Nebraska when the air sat upon me like a true burden. Then in the early evening the wind would come bringing with it delicately perfumed coolness off the fields where hay had been mown in the afternoon—it was like being resurrected. The spirit arose out of its stifling tomb and saw all things in a new and different light—it became alive. That is what I long for now—that sense of physical aliveness that pushes against the frame, enervates the flesh, that makes one feel as though even the skeletal mass is expanding and growing.

Today what joy to praise three marvelous women, and to rejoice that their paths have crossed mine. ❦

On What Becomes
of the Brokenhearted
Chuck Lathrop

All sorts of things need breaking:
seals on letters
husks on corn
bread
butterflies from cocoons
chickens from eggs
and hearts

To break a heart
Is to let me out
and let you in
To be brokenhearted
to say YES
to cracked open wideness

Heartquakes

And walking around
in my into pieces self
revelations abound
so much more room
so much more me

Not even the sidewalks can resist
persistent dandelions

They could not have known him
in the breaking of the bread
had not their hearts broken as well

Loving is breaking
into pieces
into ourselves
into each other

Heartbreakers All.

🌾

Teresa of Avila's Way
J. Mary Luti

Even friendship between two holy persons is not without a shadow side, as the following selection testifies. A classical spiritual friendship, it represents the very human experiences of Teresa of Avila, a sixteenth-century Carmelite, in her relationship with Gracián (Jeronimo de la Madre de Dios), her confessor and co-worker in the reform of Carmelite monasteries in Spain. Lest the selection seem to convey a nonreciprocal relationship, let the words of one of the many biographies of Teresa dispel this erroneous notion that theirs was merely a penitent–confessor relationship:

> Gracián was as powerfully drawn to the spirit of La Madre [Teresa] as she was to his. "She communicated her spirit to me," he wrote, "without concealing anything, and I declared all my interior to her in the same way."

DURING THE FOLLOWING SIX YEARS, the discalced leaders and pioneers found themselves drawn increasingly into an escalating struggle to retain control of the reform, at times caught in, at times shrewdly manipulating the competing royal, papal, and Religious Order jurisdictions and interests at issue in the protracted fight. Gracián fought too, giving himself over totally to this rescue of the reform, enduring repeated slander and a brief period of house arrest. He played a major role in finally securing a separate province for the discalced, and governed it as first provincial superior. With Teresa he founded new houses; he directed souls, preached, wrote, and planned. Teresa believed that he was doing incalculable good, and her love for him, the servant of the reform, kept pace.

The character of that love, however, ought not to be romanticized. Teresa had to defend it not only against those who saw in it something other than angels ascending together to the realms of light, not only from the sniping of priests and female companions who felt she was neglecting them as a result of her devotion to him. More than anything else, she had to defend it from her own disappointment; persevere in it when it was carelessly unrequited; keep it kindled when Gracián's actions showed that he did not know how to love with a mature affection that attended to the finer points of human need and to the subtle degrees that mark the difference between dedication and ambition, heroism and protagonism, righteousness and inflexibility.

Teresa's love for Gracián made her overestimate his worth at the outset; she continued to misjudge him and sometimes excused his obvious defects to others in unadmirable tones. But since that day when she had understood in a vision that God had joined them in a "marriage well-arranged," her love for him was inseparable from her love for the discalced reform. She saw his perfection as crucial to the reform's progress, and she kept after him. She could not give up on him any more than she could on the great ecclesial work she believed God had given her to do.

Her letters tell the story. Repeatedly she urged him to sleep; he must not kill himself with overwork. She suggested that instead he leave something for *God* to do. Reminding him of the importance of rectitude of intention, she hinted at his self-sufficiency and his tendency to substitute planning for prayer. She reprimanded him for failing to keep her properly informed, even wondering whether he was deliberately holding out on her. Poignantly she registered Gracián's neglect of her in remarks such as this:

Angela ... has no consolation [but your friendship] and ... she ... gets distressed when she thinks [her affection] is not requited ... Your Paternity must please tell that gentleman that, careless though he may be by nature, he must not be careless with her; for where there is love, it cannot slumber so long.

She felt his physical sufferings in her own flesh and worried constantly about his safety; but she had also to remind him that he was not the only one to pay the price of persecution. In fact, compared to John of the Cross, who had been kidnapped and imprisoned by the reform's opponents, Gracián had gotten off lightly. Since Gracián had become so despairing under tolerable circumstances, she wondered if he could ever have worn John's shoes. Teresa was also alarmed by the cowardice that had made him deaf to her advice to make a direct, obedient approach to the Father General after the Seville fiasco and help bring about a badly needed reconciliation.

More ominously, she warned him about the dangers of playing favorites and about how a religious superior could ill afford the inconsistent, autocratic, and headstrong behavior others noted in him. He was not to tempt fate by treating too severely the recalcitrant friars under his jurisdiction. For the sake of the reform he must learn to act strategically. She told him, too, that she was "shocked" to hear that he had arbitrarily imposed new rules upon the nuns in Valladolid and warned him never again to interfere with the minimalist Constitutions that sufficed to regulate their lives.

In the letters Teresa wrote him indefatigably, there are hints aplenty of Gracián's inability to leave well enough alone. On one occasion, when falsely accused of indecencies with women, Gracián made a fool of himself producing documents in his own defense. Teresa had begged him in vain not to dignify the accusations with a response. Breaking with her custom of speaking only well of him to others, she expressed her consternation to a collaborator: "Our Father," she wrote, "is acting unwisely and demeaning himself in the most dreadful way." Repeatedly she counseled him about his tendency to plunge innocently but recklessly into compromising situations. She urged him to respect the special character of their friendship by not reading aloud to others the intimate passages of her letters. With so little sense of proportion and so much apparent need to play the protagonist, Gracián risked causing worse troubles still for her and the movement.

Although unable on account of her sex to take a direct public role in the formation of the discalced province, Teresa acted decisively behind the scenes through friars, courtiers, and ecclesiastical officials sympathetic to her work. But most of all, she relied on Gracián. Her letters laid out what to say and when to say it, who to approach and who to avoid, what to insist upon and what to bargain over. She frequently deferred to Gracián's ideas and left many decisions in his hands but never hesitated to insist on her own vision or even tell him curtly, "Your Paternity will make a note of my wishes."

Although some wondered whether Gracián was truly the man for the moment, she continually made allowances for him, defended him, demanded special treatment for him, and commended him to all as the one thing necessary for reform. She campaigned to get him elected provincial and when he won, she praised Providence for the outcome. Teresa's letters are rich in praise of him. Many moving passages of admiration and gratitude show that Teresa doted on him, nearly exploding with happiness when he termed himself her "dear son." She even once demanded to know whether he loved her better than his own mother. With delicacy, she received his confidences about aspects of his interior life that troubled him, and with good humor she bore his occasional imperiousness. Frequently she lauded his "skill" and "shrewdness" in the affairs of the Order.

But her last communication with him is noticeably restrained and contains serious talk about failings of his that directly affected the well-being of the province. This weary letter is also her last of many recorded complaints about him for abandoning her with no justifiable reason at a time when she needed him most. So keenly did she feel his having left her "at such a time" that she lost the desire to write to him at all, "so I have not written," she told him in hurt tones, "until today, when it is unavoidable." Her marriage well-arranged had turned out to be a rocky one. The sharpness of her rebuke of him seems to indicate the depth of her resignation to a failed hope.

Gracián's behavior was but one of several personal betrayals and painful hardships that lend to Teresa's final days an air of appalling bleakness, a sense of something slipping away. But if on some levels the relationship had failed to satisfy the expectations she had placed upon it, it still managed to fulfill its purpose as a boost toward God. For Teresa the moral of the story was clear, and in that last long letter to her friend she spelled it out:

Teresa has borne it well. She was deeply disappointed that [you] did not come. We didn't tell her [the news] until now. In a way, I'm glad [you have disappointed her], because now she will start understanding that one can place but little trust in anyone but God—*and it has done me no harm either.*

Nonetheless, even this hurt and disappointed Teresa did not see in Gracián's confusing behavior toward her a reason to abandon him or the unfinished project that was their friendship. Faithfully, maybe even foolishly, she stuck by what she believed God had begun. In the same letter, at the very end, she exclaimed: "Oh, my Father, how oppressed I have been feeling lately! But the oppression passed off when I heard you were well!" Even chastened by the experience of his vacillations, the mere thought of him and of his work for the sake of their shared endeavor continued to be enough to raise her spirits.

It is not known what Gracián felt upon the receipt of this letter. We do know, however, that his decision to go south rather than accompany Teresa to Burgos deprived them both of the chance to bid each other good-bye, for a month later at Alba Teresa died. 🖊

Letter to Bertram and Ella Wolfe
Frida Kahlo

Coyoacán 1944, Mexico

Very dear Boitito and Ella,

You'll think I have suddenly *resuscitated* in this traitor world when you receive this singular missive, or that I was just pretending that "the virgin was talking to me" [meaning "playing dumb"] and that's why I hadn't paid any attention to you guys since the last time we saw each other in New York three years ago. Think what you damn well please. Even though I don't put out even a penny's worth of writing, you're always present in my thoughts.

I want to wish for <u>both of you</u> that this current year of 1944 (even though I don't like its numbering) might be the happiest and most pleasant of all that you have lived and will live. . . . OK children, here comes the interrogation: How is your health? What kind of lifestyle do you lead? Whom do you see and speak with once in a while?

Do you still remember that in Coyoacán there is a well-born dame, by all appreciated, who has not succumbed to sh—whose hope is always to see your dear *faces* some day, in this dear land called Tenochtitlán? If this is the case, *please* write soon, telling me *all the* details so that my heart can rejoice.

I'll tell you without much detail, i.e., "briefly,". . . how I am after my remarriage, the second episode in my life, that you already know about:

Health: So, so. My spine can still take a few more blows.

Love: Better than ever because there is a mutual under-standing between the spouses without getting in the way of equal freedom for each spouse in similar cases. We have elim-inated jealousy, violent arguments, and misunderstanding. There's a great deal of *dialectics* based on past experience. So say I!

Moola: Scarce amount, almost zero, but it's getting to be enough for the most urgent needs, for food, clothes, contri-butions, cigarettes, and here and there a bottle of aged "Cuervo" tequila, which costs $3.50 (for a liter).

Work: Too much for my energy, since I'm now a teacher at a painting school (increase in category, but decrease in strength). I start at 8 A.M. and get off at 11 A.M. I spend half an hour covering the distance between the school and my house = 12 noon. I organize things as necessary to live more or less "decently," so there's food, clean towels, soap, a set-up table, etc., etc. = 2 P.M. How much work!! I proceed to eat, then to the ablutions of the hands and hinges (meaning teeth and mouth). I have my afternoon free to spend on the beau-tiful art of painting. I'm always painting pictures, since as soon as I'm done with one, I have to sell it so I have moola for all of the month's expenses. (Each spouse pitches in for the maintenance of this mansion.) In the nocturnal evening, I get the hell out to some movie or damn play and I come back and sleep like a rock. (Sometimes the insomnia hits me and then I am fuc—bulous!!!)

Alcohol: I've succeeded in making my will of *steel* help me *decrease* the amount of drinking, bringing it down to two glasses *by day*. Only on *rare* occasions does the amount of consumption increase in volume, and is transformed by magic into a drunk state with its necessary morning "hang-over." But these cases are not very common or beneficial.

As for the rest of things that happen to everyone...

After 19 years, Don Diego's paternal love has been reborn, and as a result, little Lupita, *so-called* <u>Picos,</u> has been living with us for the last two years. Her <u>*mother,* big Lupe</u>, the eternal bomb, exploded <u>*against* little Lupe,</u> and such events made me into an adoptive "mommy" with her *adoptive child*. I can't complain, since the child is good to <u>Mee</u>chelangelo and more or less adapts herself to her dad's personality. Even so, my life is not ideal. From 1929 to the present, I don't remember <u>any time</u> when the Rivera couple did not have <u>at least one</u> female companion in their home. *Home, sweet home!* What changed was the nature of the company; in the past, it was closer to worldly love; now it is more filial. You know what I mean.

Well comrades, I'm leaving now. I told you a few things about my current life. I expect to get an answer right away to this unexpected, abrupt, heterogeneous, and almost surrealistic letter.

Your faithful and sure friend,
Doña <u>Frida</u>, the trickster.

Corita Kent: A Memoir

Daniel Berrigan

IT WAS IN 1959, through the good offices of Helen Kelly, president of Immaculate Heart College, that I, a newborn in such matters, was introduced to the state of mind known as California.

But let me step back a pace or two, and remove my shoes; we are on sacred turf. Our time is the mid-fifties. An east coast bishop has been dispatched west, at the behest, it was said, of our New York kingmaker, Cardinal Spellman. As shortly becomes evident by his performance, the new archbishop of Los Angeles intends to raise (formerly pacific so to speak) hackles and brows.

For a period, there was much soul searching in the community. A church militantly in pursuit, one thought, engendered introspection among the hardiest.

They brought in a psychologist for a plenary session. I was ferried westward to join in; on what basis was blessedly unclear. In any case, the meetings of minds, with the Pacific beating outside the old beach house where we foregathered—the meeting went, in the opinion of a few, from burdensome to nigh intolerable.

My sense, obscurely arrived at, was that such dissection, such autopsical pursuits, ought decently to wait on one's decease. So I fled the premises as quietly as might be, and began walking along the shore. And there, walking toward me, was Corita, likewise fleeing.

Something here, I thought, of the brooding, cherishing, mothering even, of the nest of mystery. We laughed, and let it go at that.

* * *

She was diminutive, and in the latter years, faded into frailty.

I never saw her angry or out of sorts. Though I frequently beheld her in great physical and psychic pain.

She seemed constitutionally unable to harbor a grievance.

Fame she wouldn't trade a straw for, not if the straw were spun into gold before her eyes.

This is what her friends remember, and mourn; her capacity for friendship, for them.

She knew that the times are a very breaker of bones. Friendships tore apart. No point in dwelling on this, except to dwell on her, and her struggle to keep bonds of affection intact, in her community and those beyond.

"Those beyond," including myself, never considered ourselves (never were considered) at the periphery of her affection.

Did her love for us allow of such an image; periphery, center? We all felt ourselves at center. She made certain we did. She beckoned us there, and the gesture was irresistible.

* * *

For years she was in and out of serious illness. There was a wearisome series of operations. She survived and went on with her work. To inquiries about her health, she used to say, ruefully, things like, "Some of me that was inside me is now outside me."

She would urge me to visit her gallery in NY, near the United Nations, and "choose what you want."

In 1981 she gathered her unsold works, made a great roll of them, sizzling with her signature hues, and shipped them on. "To make use of as you want, sell them, give them away."

We arranged an exhibit on the lower East Side of Manhattan, in a place known rather amorphously as a "movement gallery." The day of the opening, the Bread and Puppet Theatre performed all afternoon, in and out of three theaters, in and out of the street, with mime and song and symbols creating their version of our Plowshares trial.

In the gallery, I read poetry and we opened the Corita exhibit; all sales were to be in favor of the Plowshares defendants.

Months later, most of the art had disappeared; one presumed, into the hands of purchasers. And no report on sales or profits was ever made. To this day, no art has been returned, no proceeds accounted for.

Finally I told her of this. "Oh, that's nothing new," she said with a laugh. "It happens to me all the time."

Typical of those we love. Some live a long time, even under sentence of death. And in the joy of their presence we forget the dire sentence. We think of them as perpetually in the world, at our side. Illusion? way of coping? perhaps something of both.

In summer of '86, a friend called; Corita was back in hospital, surgery again; it looked grim.

And I thought, When hasn't it?

It was so grim this time, as to be final; the set jaw of the reaper. I thought, I must get to Boston.

She had survived the surgery, had lost considerable weight from that destitute little frame. I found her in a tiny room of an old wing of the hospital.

When I came in unannounced, bearing a flowering plant, "You make me cry," she said through tears. (She had said to a friend sometime before: "Oh, if I could only weep.")

I said, "I hope you won't have that put on my tombstone, I make my friends cry!" Then she laughed.

We had a good hour together. She was weak, but perked up wonderfully, very much herself, propped there on pillows, with her own art on the walls, undoubtedly the most cheerful thing her friends could bring.

Our talk wandered, calling up friends, occasions, the dreadful years of war.

Our recourse at those times, between bouts of arrest and jailing, was "let's have a party!"; and the only reason to hold one party, it seemed, was to plan another.

[Shortly after this visit, Corita died (1986) at the age of 68.] ❧

Letter to a Friend
R. W. Mize

The boughs hang heavy
the empty paths,
Rockfish Creek whispers
afternoon vespers:
remember the bridge
and turn where the honey-
suckle holds the rails:

the landscape slumbers,
I do not hunt or fish,
the deer feed sometimes
in gentle pastures:
it's good to let things
have their way with you,
the courage it takes
to leave well enough
alone can break men
that and the silence
September nights fill
up with:

most Thursdays I read,
Fridays I still write,
the weeds that threaten
my garden get Monday,
Tuesdays are gone soon
without much incense,
while Wednesdays seek
flowers that blossom
sometimes over night:

come soon
with old shoes and hat:
we'll wade through fields, let
crows have room to talk,
we may see monarchs
dancing near the creek,
surprise a thirsty fawn:
do not forget your
silence: see you soon.

PART THREE

IMPRESSIONS

❧

The deep grief we feel at the loss of a
friend arises from the feeling that in every
individual there is something which no
words can express, something which is
peculiarly his own and therefore irreparable.
Omne Individuum Ineffabile.

—Arthur Schopenhauer

Friendship Is like a Dance
Anne Morrow Lindbergh

A GOOD RELATIONSHIP has a pattern like a dance. . . .
Now arm in arm, now face to face, now back to back—it
does not matter which. Because they know they are partners,
moving to the same rhythm, creating a pattern together, and
being invisibly nourished by it. ❦

Calls for Special Gifting
L. Vander Kerken, S.J.

AUTHENTIC FRIENDSHIP . . . calls for an uncommon
endowment in mind and heart. . . . [The endowment is] what
one might call a feeling for friendship. . . . This feeling is a special power of empathy for all that concerns the object of the
feeling. . . . Thus . . . [the] people who have a feeling for
friendship [are they] who love to love. ❦

Surpasses Erotic Love
Allan Bloom

MONTAIGNE'S PROFOUND EXPERIENCE of both alternatives [erotic love and friendship] leads him unqualifiedly to
prefer friendship over erotic love. Erotic love takes hold of us,
as he says, by only one corner of ourselves . . . it really does
not imply the general or total fitting together that one finds
in friendship. ❦

Does Not Demand Perfection
Alexander Smith

THE TIDE OF FRIENDSHIP does not rise high on the bank of perfection. . . . My friends are not perfect—no more am I—and so we suit each other admirably. . . . We . . . bear and forebear. . . . It is one of the charitable dispensations of Providence that perfection is not essential to friendship. ❧

Occurs by Chance or Providence
C. S. Lewis

IN REALITY, a few years' difference in the dates of our births, a few more miles between certain houses, the choice of one university instead of another, posting to different regiments . . . any of these might have kept us apart. ❧

Takes Time
Georgia O'Keeffe

STILL—IN A WAY—nobody sees a flower—really—it is so small—we haven't time—and to see takes time, like to have a friend takes time. ❧

Opens Doors as in a Dream
Evelyn Waugh

PERHAPS ALL OUR LOVES are merely hints and symbols; a hill of many invisible crests; doors that open as in a dream to reveal only a further stretch of carpet and another door. ❦

Biographical Notes about the Major Contributors

———■———

Berrigan, Daniel (1922–). Jesuit priest, prize-winning poet, prolific prose writer; protester (as one of the "Catonsville Nine") against the Vietnam War; relentless advocate for justice and peace.

Brontë, Emily (1818–1848). One of three writing sisters, natives of Yorkshire, England; herself the author of one well-known novel, *Wuthering Heights.*

Davis, Charles (1923–). Once ranked as Britain's foremost Catholic theologian with an impressive repertoire of editing and writing.

Dickinson, Emily (1830–1886). Important American poet noted for deceptively simple, rhymed verse; of her 1,775 poems, all but seven were published posthumously; lived as a solitary in her father's house in Amherst, Massachusetts.

du Boulay, Shirley. Twentieth-century biographer; contributor to the London *Tablet.*

Fitzgibbons, Eleanor, I.H.M. (1909–). Contemporary American poet whose recent collected work is *At Creation's Open Door;* professor emeritus (English), Marygrove College, Detroit.

Frost, Robert (1874–1963). Recipient of four Pulitzer prizes for poetry. His first two volumes were published while he was in England. Much of his early life was spent in farming and part-time teaching.

Gray, Peter W. (1953–). Poet, musician, painter who has exhibited in the United States and abroad; studio and chaplaincy in Los Altos, California.

Hohlwein, Kathryn Joyce Jarrell (1930–   ). Native of Salt Lake City; college friend of Patricia Frazer Lamb, with whom she carried on a correspondence for ten years; married a German painter and printmaker (deceased); prolific editor, writer, teacher.

Houselander, Caryll (1901–1954). Popular British Catholic writer; illustrator of children's books. Disabled for much of her life, survivor of World War II, her books brought inspiration and consolation to adults. *This War Is the Passion*, *The Reed of God*, and *Guilt* are her best known.

Johann, Robert O. (1924–   ). Philosopher, ethician; professor of philosophy at Fordham University, also on faculties of Yale, Union Theological Seminary, and Holy Cross College; author of *The Meaning of Love*, *Building the Human*, *Love and Law*, and other books.

Kahlo, Frida (1907–1957). Mexican artist; beautiful, exotic, yet tortured woman (according to her self-portraits); prolific correspondent of singular candor.

Lamb, Patricia Frazer (1931–   ). Native of Los Angeles; developed friendship with Kathryn Joyce Jarrell Hohlwein, whom she met at the University of Utah; married an English doctor; lived in England, Africa, and northeast United States.

Lathrop, Charles. Irish poet; resident of the Dublin area; author of *Gentle Presence*.

Leroy, Pierre (1900–1992). French priest and missionary, Jesuit confrère and friend of Pierre Teilhard de Chardin; editor of *Letters from My Friend Teilhard de Chardin*.

Luti, J. Mary (1947–   ). Former full-time, now part-time faculty member of Andover Newton Theological School; specialist in Catholic reform and Christian spirituality of the sixteenth and seventeenth centuries.

McGuire, Brian P. (1946–). "A distinguished scholar of matters Cistercian" (Trappist), author of two key works on friendship: *Brother and Lover: Aelred of Rievaulx* and *Friendship and Community: The Monastic Experience, 350–1250*.

Mize, Raymond W. (1947–). Poet; published in *Pembroke, Lyricist, Cross Currents*, and *Crucible*; professor of English and drama at South Eastern Community College, Whiteville, North Carolina.

Oates, Joyce Carol (1938–). Acclaimed U.S. author of many novels, short stories, plays, essays, and poems (fourteen published collections of poetry); distinguished professor of humanities, Princeton University.

Powers, Jessica (1905–1988). A Carmelite nun, former New York journalist, writer of exquisite religious poetry widely published.

Roseliep, Raymond (1917–1983). Diocesan priest; Ph.D., Notre Dame University; professor emeritus, Loras College, Dubuque, Iowa; acclaimed poet, noted exponent of haiku in the Western idiom; widely published in book and journal media.

Sarton, May (1912–1995). An especially sensitive woman, her friendships, love of nature, and growing audience sustained her through long physical illnesses and bouts of depression; her fourteen books of poetry, eighteen novels, and eight works of nonfiction reflect her love of friends, natural beauty, and pets, especially cats.

Simon, Caroline J. (1953–). Professor of philosophy, Hope College, Holland, Michigan; author of *The Disciplined Heart,* in which she reflects deeply on friendship.

Teilhard de Chardin, Pierre (1881–1955). French Jesuit priest, philosopher, and paleontologist; in *The Phenomenon of Man*, tried to reconcile Christianity and science, and was censored; also wrote *The Divine Milieu* and *Hymn of the Universe* (poetic prose); died in New York on Easter Sunday, 1955.

Vander Kerken, L. (1910–1998). A Flemish Jesuit thinker and established scholar; author of books on aesthetics, happiness, and basic moral attitudes; his writing conveys profound insights on friendship.

Waugh, Evelyn (1907–1966). Noted British writer; wrote chiefly satire ("both elegant and biting"); his conversion to Roman Catholicism had great impact on his work. Well-known novels include *Brideshead Revisited* and *The Sword of Honor* (a World War II trilogy).

Sources

Berrigan, Daniel. "Corita Kent: A Memoir" (excerpts). Personal manuscript. Used by permission.

Bloom, Allan. *Love and Friendship.* New York: Simon & Schuster, 1993.

Brontë, Emily. "Love and Friendship." Written in 1839. Quoted in D. J. Enbright and D. Rawlinson, *The Oxford Book of Friendship.* New York: Oxford University Press, 1991.

Cumming, E. E. "open your heart" (excerpt). In *Complete Poems, 1904–1962.* Edited by George J. Firmage. New York: Liveright, 1991. Copyright 1944, © 1972, 1991 by the Trustees for the E. E. Cummings Trust. Reprinted by permission of Liveright Publishing Corporation.

Davis, Charles. "A Thing beyond Compare." *America* 112 (May 8, 1965): 667. Used by permission.

Dickinson, Emily. Untitled. In *The Complete Poems of Emily Dickinson,* edited by Thomas H. Johnson. London: Faber, 1970.

du Boulay, Shirley. "Companions on the Way." *The Tablet* 251 (June 21, 1997): 298–99. Used by permission.

Fitzgibbons, Eleanor. "To a Poet." In *At Creation's Open Door.* Nashville: Scythe Publications, 1995. Used by permission.

Frost, Robert. "A Time to Talk." In *The Road Not Taken,* edited by Louis Untermeyer. New York: Henry Holt & Co., 1951. © 1944 by Robert Frost. Copyright 1916, © 1969 by Henry Holt & Company. Reprinted by permission of Henry Holt and Company, Inc.

Gray, Peter W. Untitled poem. Personal copy. 1986. Used by permission.

Hohlwein, Kathryn Joyce. See Lamb, Patricia Frazer.

Houselander, Caryll. "A Note on Friendship." *The Letters of Caryll Houselander: Her Spiritual Legacy.* New York: Sheed & Ward, 1965. Used by permission.

Huddleston, Mary Anne. "Chaste Loving." Unpublished.

——. "Lenten Learning." Unpublished.

Johann, R. O. "The Power of Love." *America* 110 (June 13, 1964): 852. Used by permission.

Kahlo, Frida. "Letter to Bertram and Ella Wolfe" (Coyoacán, Mexico, 1944). In *The Letters of Frida Kahlo,* edited by Martha Zamora. San Francisco: Chronicle Books, 1995. Used by permission.

Koppelman, Susan. *Women's Friendships.* Norman, Okla.: Oklahoma University Press, 1991.

Lamb, Patricia Frazer, and Kathryn Joyce Hohlwein. In *Touchstones: Letters between Two Women, 1953–1964.* New York: Harper & Row, 1983. Copyright 1983 by Harper & Row Publishers. Reprinted by permission of the Hazelden Foundation, Inc.

Lathrop, Chuck. "On What Becomes of the Brokenhearted." In *A Gentle Presence.* Washington, D. C.: ADOC, 1977. © 1977 by Chuck Lathrop. Used by permission.

Leroy, Pierre. "Foreword: Memories of Teilhard." In *The Letters of Teilhard de Chardin and Lucile Swan,* edited by T. M. King and Mary W. Gilbert. Washington, D.C.: Georgetown University Press, 1991, 1993. Used by permission.

Lewis, C. S. "Friendship." In *The Four Loves.* New York: Harcourt Brace Jovanovich, 1960.

Lindbergh, Anne Morrow. "Argonautica." In *Gift from the Sea.* New York: Vintage Books, 1975. Copyright © 1955, 1975 and renewed 1983 by Anne Morrow Lindbergh. Reprinted by permission of Pantheon Books, a division of Random House, Inc.

Luti, J. Mary. "We Who Love Each Other in Christ" (excerpt). *Teresa of Avila's Way.* Collegeville, Minn.: Liturgical Press (a Michael Glazier Book), 1991. Copyright © 1991 by the Order of St. Benedict, Inc. Used by permission.

McGuire, Brian P. "Modern Friendship." In *Friendship and Community.* Kalamazoo: Cistercian Publications, 1988.

Mize, R. W. "Letter to a Friend." *Cross Currents* 46 (winter 1996/1997). Used by permission.

Oates, Joyce Carol. "An Unsolved Mystery." In *Between Friends: Writing Women Celebrate Friendship,* edited by Mickey Pearlman. Boston: Houghton Mifflin Co., 1994. Copyright © 1995 by Ontario Review, Inc. Reprinted by permission of John Hawkins & Associates, Inc.

O'Keeffe, Georgia. In Mary E. Hunt, *Fierce Tenderness: A Feminist Theology of Friendship.* New York: Crossroad, 1991.

The Oxford Annotated Bible (with Apocrypha). Revised Standard Version. New York: Oxford University Press, 1973, 1977.

Phillips, Katherine. "Between Men and Women" (excerpt). In *The Oxford Book of Friendship,* edited by D. J. Enright and D. Rawlinson. New York: Oxford University Press, 1991.

Powers, Jessica. "For a Proud Friend Humbled." In *House at Rest.* Pewaukee, Wis.: Carmelite Monastery, 1984. Used by permission.

Roseliep, Raymond. "The Friend." In *The Linen Bands.* Westminster, Md.: The Newman Press, 1961, © renewed 1983, Daniel J. Rogers. Used by permission.

Sarton, May. "Friday, June 1st" (journal entry). In *Recovering.* New York: W. W. Norton & Co., 1980; London: The Women's Press, 1997. Copyright © 1980 by May Sarton. Reprinted by permission of W. W. Norton & Company, Inc., and The Women's Press, Ltd.

Simon, Caroline J. "Can Women and Men Be Friends?" Adapted from ch. 6, "Friendship between the Sexes." In *The Disciplined Heart.* Grand Rapids, Mich.: Wm. B. Eerdmans Publishing Co., 1997, as published in *Christian Century* (Feb. 19, 1997): 188–94. Copyright © 1997 by the Wm. B. Eerdmans Publishing Company; all rights reserved. Used by permission.

Smith, Alexander. In *Friendship,* compiled by R. L. Woods. Norwalk, Conn.: C. R. Gibson Co., 1969.

Teilhard de Chardin, Pierre. In *The Letters of Teilhard de Chardin and Lucile Swan,* edited by T. M. King and Mary Wood Gilbert. Washington, D.C.: Georgetown University Press, 1991, 1993. Used by permission.

Vander Kerken, L., S. J. "Friendship." In *Loneliness and Love.* New York: Sheed & Ward, 1967. Used by permission.

Waugh, Evelyn. *Brideshead Revisited.* Boston: Little, Brown and Co., 1945.

———. "To Henry Yorke." In *The Norton Book of Friendship,* edited by Eudora Welty and Ronald A. Sharp. New York: W. W. Norton and Co., 1991. Originally published in *The Letters of Evelyn Waugh,* edited by Mark Amory. Copyright © 1980 by the Estate of Laura Waugh, 1982 by the Estate of Evelyn Waugh. Reprinted by permission of Ticknor & Fields/Houghton Mifflin Co. and Sterling Lord Literistic, Inc. All rights reserved.

Welsheimer, Helen. *Singing Drums.* New York: Dutton Publishers, 1937.